W9-CJF-969

MORE THAN A DREAM

THE RADICAL MARCH ON WASHINGTON
FOR JOBS AND FREEDOM

*Many older marchers showed their respect
for the march and its demands by dressing
as if they were going to church.*

An aerial view of the 250,000 marchers extending from the Lincoln Memorial, foreground, to the Washington Monument. Some marchers stopped at the reflecting pool, middle, to cool their feet.

Yohuru Williams and **Michael G. Long**

MORE THAN A
DREAM

THE RADICAL MARCH ON WASHINGTON FOR JOBS AND FREEDOM

FARRAR STRAUS GIROUX
NEW YORK

Farrar Straus Giroux Books for Young Readers
An imprint of Macmillan Publishing Group, LLC
120 Broadway, New York, NY 10271 • mackids.com

Our books may be purchased in bulk for promotional, educational, or business use. Please contact
your local bookseller or the Macmillan Corporate and Premium Sales Department at (800) 221-
7945, ext. 5442, or by email at MacmillanSpecialMarkets@macmillan.com.

Library of Congress Cataloging-in-Publication Data is available.

First edition, 2023
Book design by Maria W. Jenson and Mallory Grigg
Printed in the United States of America by Lakeside Book Company, Harrisonburg, Virginia

ISBN 978-0-374-39174-4 (hardcover)
10 9 8 7 6 5 4 3 2 1

I appeal to all of you to get into this great revolution
that is sweeping this nation. Get in and stay in the streets of
every city, every village and hamlet of this nation until
true freedom comes, until the revolution of 1776 is complete.

— JOHN LEWIS
AUGUST 28, 1963

CONTENTS

Young marchers in NAACP caps arriving at Union Station in Washington, DC

OUR WORDS

In our earlier book—Call Him Jack: The Story of Jackie Robinson, Black Freedom Fighter—*we included a special note about hurtful words that Robinson faced throughout his lifetime. Those same words appeared in the research and writing of this book, so we decided to return to our note and revise it for inclusion here.*

The words we choose to describe ourselves and one another can be respectful, kind, or cruel. They can make us smile and frown, laugh and cry, and cheer and jeer. They can make friends and enemies at the same time.

In choosing words for this book, we've tried to be as respectful as possible, while still presenting the challenges that Black people faced because of the color of their skin.

We use "Black American," "African American," and "Black" to describe Black people in the United States. We also typically use "white" to describe Americans of European descent. Plus, when we use the words "black" and "white," we employ them as adjectives rather than nouns, because skin color is just one part of our identity. It doesn't define everything about us.

When quoting other people's words, we've not changed or censored them. Our quotations sometimes include outdated words to describe Black people—for example, "Negro" and "colored." These words are part of our shared history, and we think it's important for readers to know about them.

Our quotations also contain hurtful words, many of which we also find repulsive, but we think it's important for readers to know—and feel—the words that white people used when trying to hurt Black Americans.

PART ONE
FIRST STEPS

Poster advertising the March on Washington Movement
led by A. Philip Randolph in the early 1940s

Bayard Rustin, right, worked with Martin Luther King, Jr., center, and Rev. Ralph Abernathy on the 1955 Montgomery bus boycott.

A MARCH FOR JOBS

Bayard Rustin was feeling out of sorts, and the dreary weather on that December day in 1962 didn't help. Temperatures ranged in the single digits, dirty snow covered the ground, and an icy wind blasted through the streets.

Wearing his crumpled overcoat, Rustin dashed down the subway steps and hopped on the train to Harlem. He was glad to be out of the bitter cold, but he still felt ill at ease, as if he was in the wrong place at the wrong time.

Yes, he liked his job as executive director of the War Resisters League, and he loved his Manhattan apartment. But deep down, the fifty-year-old Rustin wanted to *do* something else, to *be* somewhere else.

What he *desperately* wanted—but couldn't have, at least right now—was the chance to return to the epicenter of the civil rights movement.

Between 1955 and 1960, Rustin was a close adviser to Martin Luther King, Jr., teaching him about nonviolence, helping him develop tactics to overcome segregation, and writing some of his articles and speeches.

But all that came to a halt when Harlem congressman Adam Clayton Powell, Jr., threatened to tell the media that King and Rustin were lovers. It was a bald-faced lie. Rustin was gay, King was straight, and the two were not a couple.

But King worried. What would happen if the press published the false story? Would it hurt his reputation? Would it undermine the civil rights movement? King asked himself these questions because he knew that many people in 1960 saw gay men as psychologically sick, criminal, and immoral.

King was so terrified of potential damage that he cut Rustin out of his inner circle. The brutal act devastated Rustin, and ever since then, he had not quite found his footing.

Rustin stepped off the train in central Harlem and headed to the office of his beloved mentor, A. Philip Randolph, the only civil rights leader who had stood by his side for the past two years.

Randolph was well-known to Black people across the country. In 1925, he had founded the Brotherhood of Sleeping Car Porters, the

The Brotherhood of Sleeping Car Porters, founded by Randolph in 1925, quickly became the most powerful Black labor union in the nation.

nation's largest all-Black labor union, to secure better wages and working conditions for train workers. His efforts paid off, and he was hailed as a hero.

Then, fifteen years later, shortly before the United States entered World War II, the labor leader acquired legendary status by squaring off against President Franklin Roosevelt.

On September 27, 1940—with the war raging in Europe and Asia and America's involvement seeming possible—Randolph and two other Black leaders traveled to the White House. Their mission was to urge the president to desegregate the military and defense industries—the research facilities and factories that produced rifles, tanks, ships, and other war-related items.

Roosevelt "promised to look into possible methods of lessening, if not destroying, discrimination against Negroes." But just two weeks later, the president's press secretary issued a statement that reaffirmed racial segregation in the military. Equally troubling, there was no statement about desegregating defense industries.

Randolph was furious. But rather than seeking another Oval Office meeting, he came up with a radical idea—*an all-Black march on Washington!* The labor leader shared his idea in an article published in Black newspapers across the country.

"I suggest," he wrote, "that 10,000 Negroes march on Washington, D.C., the capital of the nation, with the slogan: WE LOYAL NEGRO-AMERICAN CITIZENS DEMAND THE RIGHT TO WORK AND FIGHT FOR OUR COUNTRY."

The march would "wake up and shock the nation's political leaders," he added. "Nobody expects 10,000 Negroes to get together and march

NEGRO AMERICA!

There's A Job For You Now . . .

We're tired of a lot of talk with no action to back it up, this is what we're going to do about it!

JOIN IN THE
March On Washington For
Jobs and Equal Participation
In National Defense
J U L Y   1 s t

This means your security . . . your right to earn a decent living.
This is a crisis for the whole of Negro America with thousands of others you will march through the streets of the nation's capitol. You will take part in the huge mass meeting at the foot of the Lincoln Memorial. Yours will be a part of the voice of Negro America lifted in resounding protest against unfair discrimination against one-tenth of the nation's population. That's us!

•

No One Will Do It For Us
We Have To Help Ourselves!

WE WILL MARCH . . .

On July 1, Black Americans coming from all parts of the country - will march from the Nation's Capitol down Constitution Avenue, past the White House and the War Department to the Lincoln Memorial where President Roosevelt has been asked to answer the mightiest protest ever made by a loyal minority group.

The march will be a silent, dignified, determined challenge to the democracy for which we have fought through the centuries. All Negroes will march! Laborers, Domestics, Mechanics, Professionals will join together that America and the world may know and heed a solemn and determined . . .

FIGHT FOR
REAL DEMOCRACY!

•

JOIN NEGRO MARCH
FOR
JOBS and JUSTICE

A promotional flyer for the 1941 march promises "a silent, dignified, determined" protest

anywhere for anything at any time. Negroes . . . are supposed to be just scared and unorganizable."

Twenty-nine-year-old Bayard Rustin was so excited by his mentor's idea that he worked full-time on recruitment. Randolph soon predicted that marchers would number not ten thousand but a hundred thousand.

Roosevelt surrendered.

On June 25, 1941, six days before the march, the president signed Executive Order 8802, which declared: "There shall be no discrimination in the employment of workers in defense industries and in Government, because of race, creed, color, or national origin."

Roosevelt's historic order marked the first time that a threatened Black protest resulted in federal action benefiting Black lives.

The *Pittsburgh Courier,* one of the nation's most important Black newspapers, celebrated the order as a "great forward step toward true national unity."

Randolph was delighted, and though he had not achieved the desegregation of the armed forces, he called off the march.

Twenty-one years later, the idea of a march was back. Now seventy-three years old, Randolph welcomed Rustin in from the cold. Both men looked forward to these regular chats about racial justice, especially since they were no longer front and center in the civil rights movement.

As Rustin took off his overcoat, Randolph settled into his high-backed leather chair. He spoke in a clipped, sophisticated accent, and while he sounded like royalty, he always took aim at inequality and injustice.

This time Randolph focused on "the biggest crisis currently facing the

A. Philip Randolph, November 1942

June 10, 1941

A. Philip

My dear Mr. ∧Randolph:

I have talked over your letter with the President and I feel very strongly that your group is making a very grave mistake at the present time to allow this march to take place. I am afraid it will set back the progress which is being made, in the Army at least, towards better opportunities and less segregation.

I feel that if any incident occurs as a result of this, it may engender so much bitterness that it will create in Congress even more solid opposition from certain groups than we have had in the past.

I know that crusades are valuable and necessary sometimes, but undertaken when the temper is as tense as it is at present, seems to me unfortunate, and to run the risk which a meeting such as this carries with it, is unwise. You know that I am deeply concerned about the rights of Negroppeople, but I think one must face situations as they are and not as one wishes them to be. I think this is a very serious decision for you to take.

Very sincerely yours,

White House file copy of Eleanor Roosevelt's June 1941 letter to A. Philip Randolph. The first lady supported racial equality, but she also opposed the 1941 march. Like many others, she believed that the march might provoke violence and create backlash in congress. Randolph would hear the same criticism when planning the 1963 march.

American Negro"—racial discrimination in employment. He was especially upset that white factory owners were replacing Black workers with machines.

The federal government *must* step in, Randolph asserted.

Randolph and Rustin were fervent socialists.

They believed that the government had a moral obligation to steer the nation's economy so that the basic needs of all people—food, shelter, education, and health care—would be met at every point in their lives. In the field of employment, for example, the government should train displaced workers, create jobs for all the unemployed, and make employers pay decent wages.

As *Black* socialists, Randolph and Rustin also believed that the government should punish businesses, industries, and labor unions that discriminated against Black people.

And as *experienced* socialists, they knew that the government would intervene in the economy only if forced to do so by a powerful social movement, like the March on Washington Movement in 1941.

CAPITALISM AND SOCIALISM

Capitalists believe in the right to private property. Socialists call for some property, like factories, to be held in common, by the government or associations of workers. Capitalists say that the economy operates best when the government doesn't interfere with it. Socialists urge the government to build an economy that serves everyone's basic needs. Capitalists argue that

SPA logo, from a 1915 brochure

business and industry owners can best serve society by earning profits. Socialists claim that the pursuit of profit alone creates an unequal society where rich people rule over poor people.

Randolph had an idea.

Let's march on Washington for jobs! We've been talking about this for more than twenty years. Let's finally do it!

Rustin lit up.

Yes! And get the entire civil rights movement to join us!

For Randolph and Rustin, it wasn't good enough for the movement to focus on desegregating trains and buses, water fountains and restrooms, stores and restaurants.

After all, what good is it to sit in a desegregated restaurant if you don't have money to buy a hamburger?

If the movement wanted *total* freedom, it had to fight for *massive* changes to an economy that discriminated against Black people. It had to fight for jobs!

Randolph lit up, too.

Bayard, we can win this!

Remembering his 1941 victory, Randolph was confident that the movement could indeed win this new fight exactly because it had the most important ingredient for any political battle—*people*!

But first things first.

Randolph asked Rustin if he'd put together a short proposal for a march that would take place the following year, in 1963, to mark the centennial of the Emancipation Proclamation and protest the nation's ongoing resistance to Black freedom.

Thrilled beyond measure, Rustin couldn't agree fast enough.

Grabbing his overcoat, he headed back into the cold air, his long chin leading the way, trusting that the brutal December winds were no match for the winds of change about to sweep across the nation.

The plans for a new march on Washington were underway.

WHY WAIT SO LONG TO ORGANIZE THE MARCH?

Although plans for a Washington march for jobs crystallized in December 1962, Randolph had spoken of the idea at least ten months earlier. If Black unemployment was "becoming a real threat," as Randolph said in a February 1962 interview, why do you think he waited so long to begin making concrete plans?

Preamble

1) The one hundred years since the signing of the Emancipation Proclamation have witnessed no fundamental government action to terminate the enconomic subordination of the American Negro. Today the ratio of unemployment among Negroes and whites remains two-to-one, while the income of Negroes is roughly half that of whites. Not only have these disparities remained constant over decades, but in the present period they have absolutely widened. Their effect on race relations generally can only frustrate the limited gains recently registered in school integration and in equal accommodations in public facilities and transportation.

2) The condition of Negro labor is inseparable from that of white labor; the immediate crisis confronting black labor grows out of the unresolved crisis in the national economy. History shows that the peculiar disadvantages suffered by the Negro as the result of segregation and discrimination are alleviated in times of relatively full employment and aggravated when unemployment is high. So far the federal government has produced no serious answers to the problem of rising unemployment; each succeeding recession has produced an upward revision of minimal unemployment rates, and Congress and the White House appear complacent in the face of current unemployment figures of 6%.

3) The current crisis is overwhelmingly the result of structural unemployment. Thousands of workers have been displaced by automation, rendered economically functionless in modern industrial society. Negroes have been disproportionately victimized, for automation has attacked precisely those unskilled and semiskilled jobs to which Negroes have traditionally been relegated. Moreover, the persistence of racial discrimination on a national scale has closed to Negroes, who have lacked the training to compete for skilled jobs, even the limited opportunities for job retraining available to whites. Statistics speak clearly: 25% of the long-term unemployed are Negroes.

4) Automation coupled with a tremendous population increase is seriously limiting job opportunities for all youth particularly Negroes in the 16-21 age group. 50% of Negro youth, 16-21 are idle. A disproportionate number of the 8,000,000 school dropouts a year are Negroes.

5) These indisputable facts dictate certain strategies for the overall progress of the Negro in the present period:

   a) Integration in the fields of education, housing, transportation and public accommodations will be of limited extent and duration so long as fundamental economic inequality along racial lines persists. Already the slowdown in the rate of progress in many of these fields is evident in the widespread characterization of recent gains as "tokenism". An economically disprivileged people is not able to utilize institutions and facilities geared to middle-class incomes in an inflated economy. They cannot afford to patronize the better restaurants, integrated or not; their own financial circumstances segregate them from middle-class housing; they cannot afford to travel, whether buses are integrated or not, or send their children to college.

   b) The demand for "merit hiring" practices is obsolete. When a racial disparity in unemployment has been firmly established in the course of a century, the change-over to "equal opportunities" merely prevents a further divergence in the relative status of the races but does not wipe out the cumulative handicaps of the Negro worker. In addition, "equal opportunities"

From its very first lines, the January 1963 march proposal builds a powerful argument.

2

A MARCH FOR JOBS—AND FREEDOM

Tom Kahn, a young white socialist, typed furiously, almost as fast as the ideas ricocheted around Bayard Rustin's cramped apartment. *Jobs for everyone! Raise the minimum wage! More job training!*

Norman Hill, a young Black socialist, chimed in with ideas about protests. *Let's have sit-ins! And shut down Congress!*

It was a gathering in late December 1962 or early January 1963. The three friends exploded with creativity for hours, developing and improving and polishing the proposal that A. Philip Randolph had requested. The result of their human Big Bang was a radical scheme to force the government to reshape the economy.

The three-page proposal focused on economic injustice and government inaction as the most important problems facing Black Americans.

"The one hundred years since the signing of the Emancipation Proclamation have witnessed no fundamental government action to terminate the economic subordination of the American Negro," the trio wrote.

Compared to white workers, Black workers suffered from high unemployment rates, low wages, and little access to job training programs. But the problem of economic justice was also more than a *Black* issue, the trio noted. There simply weren't enough good jobs for *everyone*.

The three friends called for "a two-day action program" that would demand "the emancipation of all labor" by "the creation of more jobs for all Americans."

On the first day, "a mass descent on Congress" would "so flood all Congressmen with a staggered series of labor, church, civil rights delegations from their own states that they would be unable to conduct business on the floor of Congress for an entire day." On the second day, "a mass protest rally" would take place at a location yet to be determined.

THE EMANCIPATION PROCLAMATION

In the first two years of the Civil War (1861–62), President Lincoln refused to depict slavery as a major cause of the conflict between the Union and the Confederacy, partly because he wanted to maintain the support of border states that allowed for slavery—for example, Delaware and Maryland. But on January 1, 1863, Lincoln issued the Emancipation Proclamation, an executive order that freed "all persons held as slaves" within those states that were in active rebellion against the Union. The proclamation did not free slaves in states that supported the Union or in Confederate states that were under Union control.

An 1864 engraving of a painting that imagines Lincoln signing the Emancipation Proclamation at a table on which a Bible rests.

In 1865, the Thirteenth Amendment to the Constitution finally ended chattel slavery in the United States.

With the proposal in hand, Rustin headed back to Randolph's office.

As he shared it, Rustin was probably concerned about his mentor's reaction, especially because the trio's plan called for people of all colors to take part in the protest. That was different from the all-Black march that Randolph had envisioned in 1941. But it was in line with Randolph's more recent efforts to form coalitions with labor unions and religious groups.

Randolph read the document with extra care. He'd once been a magazine editor, and he always read with a critical eye.

Then he delivered his verdict: He liked it. Very much.

Rustin breathed a sigh of relief. He thought the world of his mentor—he always called him "Mister Randolph"—and winning his approval meant a lot.

Plan D. C. 'Pilgrimage' To Reveal Jobless Crisis

BAL HARBOUR, Fla. — A mass "pilgrimage" to Washington is being planned as a means of dramatizing the "unemployment crisis" among Negroes.

Leader of the movement is A. Philip Randolph, president of the Brotherhood of Sleeping Car Porters and a vice president of the 29 - member executive council of the AFL-CIO.

Randolph is planning to call a meeting of the executive board of the Negro American Labor Council next month to complete plans for the pilgrimage. He is the head of the council, a group of Negro unionists organized several years ago to combat job bias.

Randolph, who said Negro union leaders will try to arrange a meeting with President Kennedy, cited the fact that unemployment among Negroes is more than twice as high as among whites.

A FACT

The statistics from the Labor Department showed that in January the unemployment rate among white workers was 5.9 per cent; among Negro workers it was 12.7 per cent. Added to this is the fact that a majority of the Negro unemployed are long-term cases.

Randolph cited several factors which are responsible for the employment plight of Negroes. Among them is the rapid decrease in unskilled and

(Continued On Page 6)

Randolph's use of "pilgrimage" to describe the upcoming march was short-lived. (Chicago Daily Defender, February 26, 1963)

Plan D. C.

(Continued From Page 2)

semi-skilled jobs, and the fact that Negroes are seldom able to acquire seniority and gain promotion to higher jobs.

He added, however, that automation is also helping Negro workers by breaking down old patterns of seniority and making special skills a prerequisite for many jobs.

CITE FIGURES

Statistics show that Negroes comprise 11 per cent of the population, but 24 per cent of persons who have been unemployed 15 or more weeks are Negroes, and 26 per cent of those out of work more than six months are Negroes.

Randolph has several important successes to his credit in the fight for civil rights. He called off a proposed march to Washington during World War II after President Roosevelt agreed to demands that Negroes get jobs in defense work.

Later, he told President Truman that he would urge Negroes not to serve in the armed forces as long as they were segregated. Truman hastily signed an order for integration of the services.

Randolph's record of successful protests gave credibility to his call for a new march on Washington.

Randolph offered no significant changes to the plan, and in February 1963, he began to speak in public about the need for a "pilgrimage" to Washington to protest the "unemployment crisis" suffered by Black workers.

A month later, he dropped the word "pilgrimage"—which suggested a quiet religious journey—and used the more militant-sounding "march." "And that march should include from 25,000—or better, 100,000—persons to move President Kennedy and the administration to urgency and action on the Negro job plight."

Randolph then took the proposal to the executive board of the Negro American Labor Council (NALC), an all-Black organization that fought for civil rights within the labor movement. Randolph was the leader of the NALC, and he asked council members to approve "a call for an emancipation march on Washington for jobs."

The council members voted yes, giving Randolph the credibility and traction that he needed for enlisting other civil rights leaders, including the most influential of them all—Martin Luther King, Jr.

When he first heard of the plan, King was preoccupied. He was focusing all his time and energy on leading a campaign for civil rights in Birmingham, Alabama, a city notorious for racial segregation and violence against Black people. So far, the campaign had faced stiff resistance from white leaders, and King had failed to build support among Black adults.

With few options before him, King was now considering a controversial plan to invite Black children and teenagers to join the Birmingham protest marches. He worried about placing young people in harm's way, but he also recognized that racial segregation damaged their emotional well-being every minute of their young lives.

Taking a deep breath, King approved the plan.

On the morning of May 2, 1963, Black students whispered in school hallways across the city of Birmingham, reminding one another that today was "D-Day."

Don't tell the teachers!

Go directly to the church!

At 11:00 a.m., about one thousand students ditched their classes and streamed toward Sixteenth Street Baptist Church. One principal had locked his school's gates, but the students just laughed and scaled the fence.

"We poured into Sixteenth Street like a waterfall!" a student recalled. Singing protest songs, the students assembled into groups of fifty. Around noon, they left the church one group at a time and marched toward City Hall.

White police officers arrested most of the students just after they started to march, but a few of the young protesters broke away and darted downtown.

Public Safety Commissioner Eugene "Bull" Connor—the head of Birmingham's police officers and firefighters—greeted them at City Hall, and not in a nice way. Connor did not support civil rights for

Black people, and he opposed all civil rights protests, even peaceful ones by young people.

When a boy at City Hall told Connor he wanted to kneel and pray for freedom, the safety commissioner spat in his face. Connor then instructed his officers to put all the young protesters in paddy wagons and haul them to jail.

By the end of the day, police officers had arrested 970 students, including children from elementary schools. Some of the jailed students cried; others tried to calm them. And students who had avoided arrest plotted more demonstrations the next day.

On May 3, the second day of the protest, thousands of Black students descended on Kelly Ingram Park, a public area that divided Black neighborhoods from the white downtown area. Singing and clapping and dancing, the students again protested segregation.

And again, Bull Connor fumed. The public safety commissioner barked out an order, and firefighters he'd stationed nearby aimed their supercharged hoses at the young protesters. In a matter of seconds, jets of water blasted students off their feet and pinned them against trees and walls.

Connor shouted another order, and baton-wielding police officers turned their German shepherds on the students. The snarling dogs lunged at arms and legs, backs and chests, faces and throats.

Blood-curdling screams filled the air.

Photographs and newsreels of the brutality traveled across the world, and people everywhere wondered if the United States really did stand for freedom and justice for all.

The worldwide disgust inspired Martin Luther King, Jr.

Sparking international outrage, the images of police dogs attacking Birmingham students fueled interest in the proposed March on Washington.

"We are at the point where we can mobilize all this righteous indignation into a powerful mass movement," he told an adviser in early June. King also said that it might be a good time to announce a "march on Washington," because "the threat itself may so frighten the President that he would have to do something."

Around this same time, Randolph continued to call for a march for jobs. Using his most militant language yet, he said that the time had come "for the development of a massive national effort of the black laboring masses" to march on Washington "in order to wake up Negro America to the job crisis now upon it."

Then, on June 9, King made his first public statement about the possibility of "a march on Washington, even sit-ins in Congress." Members of King's inner circle also began to speak about a protest in Washington. On June 11, one adviser told the media that unless Congress passed civil rights legislation, "thousands upon thousands of Negroes" would stage a "massive, militant and monumental sit-in" in Washington, DC.

There would also be "massive acts of civil disobedience all over the nation." Civil rights activists "will tie up transportation by laying our bodies prostrate on runways of airports, across railroad tracks and at bus depots."

That night, President John F. Kennedy appeared on television and called upon Congress to pass a civil rights law that would give "all Americans the right to be served in facilities which are open to the public—hotels, restaurants, theaters, retail stores, and similar establishments."

Looking directly into the camera, the president also praised Birmingham's student protesters. "Like our soldiers and sailors in all parts of the world, they are meeting freedom's challenge on the firing line, and I salute them for their honor and their courage."

As King listened to the speech, tears of joy ran down his face. Yet although he was grateful, the civil rights leader also recognized that members of Congress would never pass a civil rights bill unless they were forced to do so.

So King called A. Philip Randolph with a proposal: *Let's combine our ideas and march on Washington for jobs and desegregation.*

On June 18, the two leaders met in Randolph's office for more than three hours to discuss plans for a combined march. At the end of the meeting, their representatives held a press conference to announce that

"100,000 or more Negroes" would march on Washington and that tentative plans called for a massive rally at the Lincoln Memorial. The purpose of the march would be to support President Kennedy's civil rights bill and to secure jobs for all people.

In his own comments to reporters, Randolph stressed the urgency of a march for jobs. "There will be job riots all over the nation," he said, "unless steps are taken now to reduce the high rate of unemployment." Joblessness had created a situation of "explosive social dynamite."

Now was the time to march!

3

KENNEDY RESISTS

The news report that one hundred thousand Black Americans would march on Washington shocked the White House. President Kennedy was not happy at all. He thought the march would intimidate Congress and that members would withdraw their support for the new civil rights bill. He also feared that if the march turned violent, it would sink any chance to pass the bill.

The president planned to share his displeasure at an upcoming meeting with thirty leaders in the civil rights movement. The invitation list to the prestigious gathering included a group of men known as the "Big Six"—A. Philip Randolph of the Negro American Labor Council (NALC), Martin Luther King, Jr., of the Southern Christian Leadership Conference (SCLC), Roy Wilkins of the National Association for the Advancement of Colored People (NAACP), Whitney Young of the National Urban League (NUL), James Farmer of the Congress of Racial Equality (CORE), and John Lewis of the Student Nonviolent Coordinating Committee (SNCC). They were called the *Big* Six because they led and represented arguably the most important civil rights organizations in the nation.

THE CIVIL RIGHTS ACT OF 1963

On June 19, 1963, President Kennedy sent his civil rights bill to Congress. The proposed legislation prohibited discrimination based on race and sex in employment. It also barred discrimi-

nation in federally funded programs and in public accommodations like stores and restaurants. Further, it sought to ensure
the enforcement of voting rights and the desegregation of public
schools. The bill faced stiff resistance in Congress from socially
conservative Republicans and Democrats, especially those from
the South.

Introduced June 19, 1963, the Senate version of
what would become the Civil Rights Act of 1964
listed forty-six senators as sponsors.

On June 22, a White House staffer escorted the group of thirty
into the Cabinet Room. The guests milled about nervously, wondering

who would sit where, and Vice President Lyndon Johnson soon joined them.

"It was mind-blowing for me to be there," said John Lewis, the young leader of the Student Nonviolent Coordinating Committee.

Lewis noticed that President Kennedy was in a rush as he strode into the room. Cordial and mannerly, the president greeted everyone before taking a seat and beginning his remarks.

With Martin Luther King, Jr., on his right, the president talked about the challenges of passing the civil rights bill. Perhaps the biggest obstacles were members of his own party—Dixiecrats, white Southern Democrats who opposed racial integration.

Roy Wilkins, the head of the NAACP, offered to help lobby members of Congress, and the president silently nodded his approval.

Up until this moment, no one had broached the controversial topic at hand—the proposed march on Washington. But the elephant in the room was about to roar.

Whitney Young, the leader of the National Urban League, asked President Kennedy whether he opposed the march. Without delay, the president went on the offensive.

"We want success in the Congress, not a big show," the president said in a pointed tone. "It seemed to me a great mistake to announce a march on Washington before the bill was even in [a congressional] committee. The only effect is to create an atmosphere of intimidation—and this may give some members of Congress an out."

A. Philip Randolph would have none of it.

"Mr. President, the Negroes are already in the streets," Randolph countered. "It is very likely impossible to get them off. If they are bound to be in the streets in any case, is it not better that they be led by organizations dedicated to civil rights and disciplined by struggle rather than to leave them to other leaders who care neither about civil rights nor about nonviolence?"

That was an unmistakable threat. Randolph didn't identify who the "other leaders" were, but everyone understood that he was referring to Malcolm X, the Nation of Islam minister who often ridiculed civil rights leaders for using nonviolence and pursuing integration. Malcolm believed that Black people had a right to defend themselves with force and that white people would never accept Black people as equal members of society. The Kennedy administration constantly feared that Malcolm or someone like him would spark violent uprisings against the government.

"There *will* be a march," Randolph declared.

Kennedy stood his ground. "To get the votes we need, we have, first, to oppose demonstrations which will lead to violence, and, second, give Congress a fair chance to work its will."

Vice President Lyndon Johnson added that the best way to influence lawmakers was by using "the traditional American way"—lobbying.

But Martin Luther King, Jr., wouldn't give in, either.

The march, he said, "could serve as a means through which people with legitimate discontents could channel their grievances under disciplined, nonviolent leadership . . . It may seem ill-timed. Frankly, I have never engaged in any direct-action movement which did not seem ill-timed."

Exasperated, Kennedy left the meeting at the ninety-minute mark.

Leaving the White House, the Big Six stopped to talk with reporters. King said that while Kennedy had questions about the march, he did not demand that they cancel it.

'WE CAN'T STOP NOW,' JFK TOLD

(FULL TEXT OF MESSAGE, Pg. 11)
WASHINGTON
While enthusiastic in their praise

for President Kennedy's far-reaching civil rights proposals, leaders Saturday flatly turned down his call for an

The unanimous rejection was voiced

at the White House by the NAACP's Roy Wilkins, Dr. Martin Luther King of the Southern Christian Leadership

Conference, James Farmer of CORE, Whitney Young of the National Urban League, and A. Philip Randolph, pres-

—'We can't stop'

(Continued from Page 1)

It was Mr. Randolph who informed Attorney General Robert Kennedy of plans to go through with the march of 100,000 citizens from all over the nation on the Capitol when Congressional debate on the program gets underway.

MR. KENNEDY, in asking a moratorium on demonstrations, expressed the opinion that they would do more harm than good in winning Congressional approval of the sweeping civil rights package he proposed last week.

The leaders were firm in turning down the President's request.

Said Mr. Farmer, speaking for CORE: "We do not intend to call off demonstrations, and we would not if we could.

"We do not agree that demonstrations for freedom will damage the chances of the passage of civil rights legislation." The demand for freedom is not something that can be turned on and turned off."

MR. WILKINS, NAACP secretary, sharing Mr. Farmer's opinion, pointed out that demonstrations "are a part of the American tradition of protest."

"I am certain," he said, "that demonstrators will be guided by their reactions to conditions existing in their own communities."

He also endorsed the proposed march on Washington as a protest against a certain Southern filibuster.

Dr. Martin Luther King also was forthright in his rejection of the Administration plea for a cessation of demonstrations.

Earlier he had warned that if Southern legislators attempted to filibuster to block legislation, the massive march on the Capitol would be held.

JULIAN BOND, speaking for the Student Non-Violent Coordinating Committee, declared:

"We cannot, in good conscience, ask American citizens who have been denied their rights for 300 years to refrain from voicing their demands in any way they choose.

"We believe the continuation of protests will not hinder the passage of civil rights legislation, but will, in fact, serve to point out the pressing need for it."

WHITNEY YOUNG, executive director of the National Urban League, generally a less militant organization, also expressed unwillingness to go along with a halt to demonstrations.

Guichard Parris, public relations director for the League, earlier had said: "I don't believe a so-called armistice on demonstrations is a reasonable request, because in the past there have been no demonstrations and, in spite of that, Congress failed to react."

Bishop Smallwood E. Williams, chairman of the Washington chapter of the Southern Christian Leadership Conference, and a leader of last week's mass march in the capital, was also adamant.

"The President is acting in good faith," he conceded, "but we can't commit ourselves to stop because of the attitude of Dixiecrats and reactionary Republicans.

"I think Congress has been holding a sit-in demonstration for generations on civil rights. We can't sit idly by while they resort to the same old sit-in game of filibuster."

WHILE PRESIDENT KENNEDY failed to win approval of his plea for a moratorium, North Carolina liberal Gov. Terry Sanford met with greater success in a similar request.

Kelly M. Alexander, of Charlotte, president of the North Carolina state conference of NAACP branches, Wednesday asked 96 member branches to cease demonstrations at the governor's request.

His plea was also directed to NAACP Youth Councils, which have been bearing the brunt of the demonstrations all over the state.

Alexander added that he wanted to make clear that his request "should not be construed to mean that peaceful demonstrations will permanently cease."

THERE WAS also some question whether representatives of CORE, the Southern Christian Leadership Conference and the Student Non-Violent Coordinating Committee would be governed by Alexander's suggestion.

Gov. Sanford's moratorium request was contained in an address in which he pointed out that civil rights leaders had got across their message and further demonstrations would "serve no good purpose."

He appointed Maj. Gen. Capus Waynick of High Point, a former U.S. Ambassador and state adjutant general to represent him working with mayors for racial peace.

The governor also invited protest leaders to meet with him in the state capitol at Raleigh this week for a discussion of their problems.

MEANWHILE CONGRESS was moving with all deliberate speed to consider Mr. Kennedy's sweeping proposals.

Hearings were scheduled for Tuesday by the Senate Commerce Committee on the equal public accommodations section of the omnibus bill.

It is this section which is meeting with the greatest opposition from conservative Republicans, including Minority Leader Everett Dirksen and GOP presidential hopeful, Barry Goldwater.

Goldwater, hoping to win Southern support in his candidacy, at first had voiced opposition to any civil rights legislation.

Friday he modified this position and centered his opposition on the public accommodations angle. But he did say he would never vote for cloture to cut off Dixiecrat filibusters against the proposals.

IN THE HOUSE, Chairman Emanuel Celler of the Judiciary Committee, announced that his committee would begin hearings on the Kennedy package on Wednesday.

The Administration is hopeful to secure House passage of the measures before the Senate acts. The bills face only the hurdle of the Rules Committee, headed by Virginia's Howard Smith in the House.

But in the Senate, in addition to the certain Dixie filibuster, the measures must pass through the recalcitrant hands of the Senate Judiciary Committee, headed by Mississippi's James O. Eastland.

The committee for the first time has a majority of members who favor civil rights legislation, which is expected to cripple Eastland's delaying tactics somewhat.

SPECIFICALLY, the Chief Executive asked for enactment of the following programs:

1. Legislation compelling states which have literacy tests to accept the completion of a sixth grade in a recognized public or private school (whether state-accredited or not) as a "presumption" that an applicant is qualified to vote.

2. Legislation prohibiting racial discrimination in public places such as theaters, restaurants, hotels, motels, tourist homes, and stores. Such services must be made available, regardless of race, to interstate as well as local customers.

3. Laws giving the government added authority in assisting the orderly desegregation of schools and making federal financial aid available to school districts in the throes of desegregation.

THE ATTORNEY GENERAL would be able to go to the courts and seek injunctive action, but the courts would issue only equity orders which would carry no fines or convictions.

4. Provisions for the setting up of a Community Relations Service charged with resolving disputes, disagreements, or difficulties relating to discriminatory practices based on race.

Pending action by Congress, the President promised to set up such a service by executive order.

5. Legislation giving the government authority to withold federal assistance to contractors and subcontractors who discriminate in employment on the ground of race, color, religion or national origin...

6. Authority to make the President's Committee on Equal Employment Opportunity a permanent body and rename it the "Commission on Equal Employment Opportunity."

THE FUNCTION of the Commission would be to "prevent discrimination against employees or applicants for employment ... by government contractors and subcontractors."

Included in the proposals was a provision to expand the work of the civil Rights Commission and make the agency a "clearing house" for civil rights information.

Black newspapers highlighted the opposition to President Kennedy's hope that the Big Six would call off the march. (Afro-American, June 29, 1963)

"We made it clear that we did not intend to have a violent demonstration," King said. "We feel a demonstration would help the President's civil rights legislation, would help dramatize the issue."

Roy Wilkins refused to back King. When asked about the march, the NAACP leader said, "That little baby does not belong to me."

A behind-the-scenes showdown was about to happen.

The Big Six then headed to a lunch hosted by Walter Reuther, the white president of the United Auto Workers. He had attended the White House meeting and was a staunch supporter of both the civil rights movement and President Kennedy.

The lunch soon became a negotiating session, with Wilkins expressing his wariness about the march. "I favored the quiet, patient lobbying tactics that worked best on Congress," he said later.

On the other side, King preferred not only a march but also sit-ins and other acts of civil disobedience. Wilkins bristled at the mention of disruptive sit-ins; such actions, he believed, would create a backlash against the bill.

After an intense discussion, Wilkins and King agreed to meet in the middle—to work together on lobbying and a march *without civil disobedience.* No sit-ins in Congress. No lying on airport runways. No stretching across railroad tracks. Not a hint of lawbreaking.

NONVIOLENT PROTESTS AND THE BIG SIX

Nonviolent direct-action protests—for example, marches, sit-ins, and picketing—were prominent in the civil rights movement, but they were not popular among everyone in the Big Six. Roy Wilkins preferred lobbying and filing court cases, and Whitney Young liked building social programs in urban areas. Although Wilkins and Young didn't oppose nonviolent protests, they didn't see them as the best tactics for their own work. By contrast, A. Philip Randolph, James Farmer, Martin Luther King, Jr., and John Lewis embraced nonviolent protests as essential and effective methods for advancing civil rights. They didn't dispute the importance of lobbying, filing court cases, and building social programs, but they focused much of their time and energy on using nonviolent protests.

Young students holding a sit-in to oppose racial discrimination at Katz Drug Store, Oklahoma City, August 26, 1958

As King saw it, the compromise was worth it. Yes, it would infuriate SNCC (pronounced *snick*) and CORE militants who were experts in civil disobedience and used it frequently and effectively. But the compromise meant that the march now had the support of the NAACP, the largest, most organized, and wealthiest civil rights group in the nation.

Of course, it also meant that Wilkins now had a say in decisions about the march, including the all-important appointment of the march director. If Wilkins had his say, the director would not be the obvious candidate—Bayard Rustin.

4

CHOOSING THE DIRECTOR

Back in his NAACP office, Roy Wilkins telephoned Rustin.

"Look, Bayard, I want you to know that I'm not in favor of your organizing the March on Washington."

Wilkins's words hurt—*a lot*. Planning protests was Rustin's specialty, and he craved the chance to organize what might be the largest demonstration in US history.

"There are several reasons," Wilkins explained. "First of all, I know that you were a sincere conscientious objector during the war, but you have been called a draft dodger . . . Second, you are a socialist, and many people think that socialism and communism are the same thing. Thirdly, you admit that you belonged to the Young Communist League. And then there's the whole business of your having been arrested in California on a sex charge."

Wilkins was right. In the late 1930s, Rustin worked for racial justice as a member of the Young Communist League. During World War II, he was imprisoned for refusing to serve in the military. In 1953, he was arrested for having sex in a car. And, to top it off, he was still a diehard socialist.

All that was problematic, according to Wilkins, because most people in the United States opposed communism, embraced capitalism, honored military service, and disapproved of homosexuality. If they learned about Rustin's past, they might see the march as un-American or anti-American.

"I know, I know," Rustin replied. "But what happens depends on you

Jail Rustin 60 Days On Morals Rap

PASADENA, Calif. — Bayard Rustin, 40, prominent lecturer and fearless fighter for civil rights, was sentenced to 60 days in county jail on a morals charge last week, on a guilty plea.

The inside of jails are nothing new to Rustin, but on previous occasions he saw them for refusing to bow to Jim Crow laws in many Southern states.

He was arrested by Pasadena police early last Thursday in

Rayard Rustin

company with two white men in an auto parked near a hotel. The other men, Marvin W. Long, 23, and Louie Buono, 23, were given similar sentences. Sexual deviates are often referred to as "queers."

Rustin has traveled extensively in America and abroad. He returned to this country in early October from a tour of Africa. His arrest interrupted a speaking tour for the Fellowship of Reconciliation and the American Friends Service Committee.

Jailed Before Speech

A delegation of three members of the American Friends society appeared in court, but did not testify in Rustin's behalf. The lecturer was sentenced on the eve of a scheduled address before the Quaker group at the Pasadena First Methodist church.

people who are the main leaders. If you stand up and have some courage, it will do no damage."

On July 2, the Big Six gathered at the Roosevelt Hotel in Midtown Manhattan for the first official march meeting. By this point, all six had committed to the protest.

A. Philip Randolph opened the meeting by sharing his long-time dream of a massive march on Washington—and his hope that Bayard Rustin would direct it.

Wilkins immediately objected to Rustin, ticking off the reasons he'd mentioned in his earlier call. After an intense back-and-forth, the group finally settled on Randolph as the director and Rustin as the deputy director.

The arrangement still irked Wilkins, and he delivered a final warning to Randolph. "You can take [Rustin's past] on if you want," he

When choosing the march director, the Bix Six discussed Rustin's 1953 arrest in California. (Chicago Defender, January 31, 1953)

The Big Six—(from left) John Lewis, Whitney Young, A. Philip Randolph, Martin Luther King, Jr., James Farmer, and Roy Wilkins—at the Roosevelt Hotel on July 2, 1963

said, "but don't expect me to do anything about it when the trouble starts."

Although his title was "deputy director," Rustin had just become the main organizer for the march. He was very pleased.

Next, the Big Six turned their attention to an eight-page document that Rustin had prepared for the meeting—"Proposed Plans for March." The new proposal was quite different from the one that A. Philip Randolph had approved almost six months earlier.

"This demonstration is a one-day affair," the new proposal stated. Rustin had nixed the two-day protest to avoid the logistical nightmare, as well as the added dangers, of one hundred thousand tired, hungry, vulnerable people trying to find places to sleep and eat.

THE COMMUNIST THREAT

In the 1950s and 1960s, the United States and the Soviet Union were engaged in a "cold war" with each other. Each accused the other of seeking world domination. The US government believed that Soviet communism, with its call to abolish private property and the right to worship freely, was a direct threat to US capitalism and democracy. President Kennedy personally warned Martin Luther King, Jr., that two of his advisers, Stanley Levison and Jack O'Dell, were communists.

The Young Communist League marching against war in 1935

Although shortened from two days, the protest would still be packed full of action.

It would include a protest for jobs at the White House, targeted lobbying of Congress, a march down Pennsylvania Avenue (and past the White House), and a mass rally at the Lincoln Memorial.

The Big Six quibbled over the details, but they agreed that the protest would be officially named the "March on Washington for Jobs and Freedom," and that it would take place the following month, on Wednesday, August 28, 1963.

After the meeting, Martin Luther King, Jr., told reporters that the march would be "the strongest action, numerically speaking, that we have ever held."

The *Chicago Defender*—a prominent Black newspaper founded in 1905—was so excited that it soon published a front-page headline boldly declaring, "300,000 TO MARCH ON CAPITAL AUG. 28."

The pressure was on. And no one felt it more acutely than the gay, pacifist, socialist ex-convict who now served as deputy director.

Bayard Rustin had just eight weeks until March Day.

WHY MARCH ON A WEDNESDAY?

If the Big Six were trying to attract as many people as possible, why did they choose to hold the march on a Wednesday? For many workers, attendance at the march would require taking a day off and losing part of their weekly paycheck. Wouldn't it have been better to hold the march on a Saturday or Sunday?

300,000 To March On Capital Aug. 28

NEW YORK — (UPI) — Roy Wilkins, executive secretary of the National Association for the Advancement of Colored People, said plans are being made for a massive march on Washington Aug. 28 in support of civil rights legislation.

Wilkins made the statement after a "summit meeting" of Negro leaders in the Hotel Roosevelt. He said the march on the capital was designed to "throw the spotlight" on the plight of Negroes in this country."

A spokesman for the Southern Christian Leadership Conference said last week that some 300,000 persons were ready to take part in any demonstration such as that which has been called.

Others attending the meeting were the Rev. Martin Luther King Jr., chairman of the Southern Christian Leadership Conference. He said the Aug. 28 demonstration in Washington would "dramatize Negro unemployment in the United States."

With Wilkins and King in the meeting were James Farner, national director of the Congress of Racial Equality; A. Philip Randolph, president of the Brotherhood of Sleeping Car Porters; Whitney Young Jr., director of the National Urban League, and John Lewis, chairman of the Student Non-Violent Coordinating Committee.

PRIVATE MEET

That group met privately and then went into session with 55 national religious, labor, business, civil, professional and fraternal groups to detail plans for the demonstration.

In Chicago earlier the NAACP threatened to work actively for the defeat of congressmen in 1964 who fail to support strong civil rights legislation.

Wilkins, in a keynote address at the NAACP's 54th annual convention, specifically named Sens. Barry Goldwater, R-Ariz., Everett M. Dirksen, R-Ill., and Richard B. Russell, D-Ga., among those who have opposed President Kennedy's civil rights program.

Wilkins spoke of the "conspiracy" to use Washington, D. C., "to continue human slavery under another name."

Wilkins told a sweltering, overflow crowd that jammed the 4,400 seats, aisles, halls and vestibule to a South Side church auditorium that Goldwater:

HITS GOLDWATER

". . . Wants what Sen. Russell wants, what Gov. Barnett of Mississippi and Gov. Wallace of Alabama want — a 'hands off' policy by the federal government with the Negro citizen left to the tender care of the Bull Conners (former Birmingham, Ala., police commissioner) of this world, to the supervision of state governments that bar him from voting and encourage public climate in which he can be murdered if he tries to vote."

If segregationists can use the capital "as their plotting ground for prejudice, we propose to use the capital as the parade ground for human rights," Wilkins told the NAACP 54th annual convention delegates.

He promised a "march for decency and dignity, a march in the softer cadence than the hoofbeats of the mount of Paul Revere, but with as clear a signal to men to rally to the cause of freedom."

The Chicago Defender, *perhaps the most militant of Black newspapers, was enthusiastic in its support for the march.* (Chicago Daily Defender, *July 3, 1963*)

Arrests of Roy Wilkins, left, and Medgar Evers, of the NAACP, in Jackson, Mississippi, June 1, 1963

5

REMEMBERING MEDGAR EVERS

Roy Wilkins was shocked. He'd never seen anything like this at an NAACP rally. Yes, there were always rowdy politics, but nothing had ever approached this level of intensity.

After the Big Six meeting, Wilkins had flown back to Chicago for an NAACP convention, and although he'd had some concerns about this event—a July Fourth rally in Grant Park—he had not predicted *this*.

Bishop Stephen Spottswood, the chair of the NAACP, tried his best to quiet the noisy crowd of thirty thousand, but the boos and jeers were unrelenting.

The bishop didn't take the outburst personally. He understood that the crowd was directing its fury at the man standing next to him— Reverend J. H. Jackson, president of the National Baptist Convention, the largest denomination of Black Baptists in the United States.

Nine days earlier, Jackson had called for a sixty-day stoppage to all civil rights demonstrations. Because the moratorium would begin on July 4, the March on Washington for Jobs and Freedom would be among the canceled protests.

Echoing President Kennedy, Jackson had claimed that the march would intimidate Congress, drive away potential allies, and possibly lead to violence. It would also deflect attention away from Medgar Evers.

Jackson's mention of Evers—an NAACP activist long respected for organizing boycotts and demonstrations, investigating the murders of

Black people, and enlisting Black voters—touched a raw nerve among NAACP supporters. They were still reeling from the awful news of June 12.

———————

On the evening of June 11, 1963, while President Kennedy was delivering his historic speech about civil rights, Medgar Evers, the NAACP's main organizer in Mississippi, was leading a meeting about fighting segregation in his adopted hometown of Jackson. The grueling meeting dragged on, and Evers did not return home until past midnight.

As Evers pulled his Oldsmobile into the driveway, his wife, Myrlie, and their three children ran to the front door, eager to welcome him home. Myrlie had let the kids stay up extra late so they could talk with their father about the president's speech.

Walking toward the house, Medgar carried a stack of sweatshirts that read, "Jim Crow Must Go."

Then, a rifle shot rang out, and Medgar collapsed.

Myrlie and the children rushed to his side. "Daddy!" the children cried. "Daddy! Daddy!" But Medgar was so badly wounded that he couldn't respond to their pleas. Myrlie fell to her knees and cradled her beloved husband.

Shortly after, neighbors lifted Medgar into a station wagon for quick transport to the hospital. "Sit me up," he muttered unexpectedly. "Turn me loose."

But within the hour, he was dead.

Several days later, police officers arrested Byron De La Beckwith, a white supremacist and segregationist, for the murder of Medgar Evers.

Many people believed that the best way to honor Evers was to continue protesting for racial justice, just as he had always done. But Reverend J. H. Jackson said that out of respect for Evers, civil rights activists should stop their protests and observe sixty days of mourning and praying.

Now, standing on the speaker's platform at the NAACP rally, Jackson planned to invite the crowd to support his call for a moratorium. But they weren't buying it. They already knew of his plan, and they were enraged.

When Bishop Spottswood held up his hands, asking for quiet, the crowd just protested louder and louder.

Myrlie Evers comforts her son Darrell at the funeral of Medgar Evers on June 15, 1963.

"Uncle Tom, go home!" they yelled, suggesting that Jackson groveled before white people.

"Jackson must go!"

After ten minutes of nonstop booing and jeering, Jackson acknowledged defeat and walked off the platform. But even that did little to quell the fury. A group of fifty surrounded the minister, yelling, "Kill him! Kill him!" Trapped against a wall, Jackson feared for his life. Finally, a team of ushers and police officers freed the minister and escorted him to his car.

The July 4 NAACP rally was an eye-opening experience.

The murder of Medgar Evers had *radicalized* civil rights activists. They were steaming mad, and they would no longer tolerate moderates who, like J. H. Jackson, wanted to slow or stop protests.

The Big Six wondered how to address the intense anger over Evers's murder.

Is there anything we can do to harness or channel it so that it doesn't explode at the march?

The question plagued them until someone in the circle of march organizers came up with a creative suggestion that flipped Jackson's plan on its head.

Let's march in memory of Medgar Evers!

The Big Six rallied around the idea and even expanded it to include others who had been murdered while fighting for civil rights.

"The parade," they announced, "will dramatize our demands for Jobs and Civil Rights and will commemorate Medgar Evers of the NAACP, Herbert Lee of SNCC, William Moore of CORE, and the thousands of nameless heroes of the freedom movement who have given their lives in the struggle for full equality."

THE MURDER OF HERBERT LEE

In September 1961, Herbert Lee was working with SNCC activist Bob Moses to register Black voters in Mississippi. Lee's daring efforts ended abruptly when E. H. Hurst, a white state legislator, murdered him in broad daylight. Hurst claimed that Lee, a Black man, had attacked him with a tire iron and that he had killed Lee in self-defense. A dozen witnesses, some coerced by the local sheriff, supported Hurst's claim, and an all-white jury acquitted him on the same day the killing took place. One of the eyewitnesses, a Black man named Louis Allen, later recanted his testimony, saying that Lee had never attacked Hurst. But Lee's killer remained free.

Herbert Lee, shown here with his wife, Prince Lee, took great risks when driving SNCC's Bob Moses on trips to recruit Black voters.

THE MURDER OF WILLIAM MOORE

In April 1963, CORE member William Moore undertook a one-person march from Chattanooga, Tennessee, to Jackson, Mississippi. His plan was to hand-deliver a letter urging Ross Barnett, the segregationist governor of Mississippi, to become an advocate for racial equality and Black freedom. But Moore never reached his destination. A suspected KKK member shot and killed him on Highway 11, about three hundred miles short of Jackson.

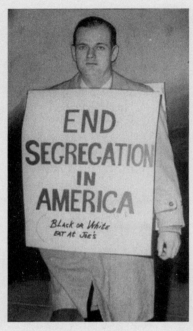

William Moore carried out several one-person protests for racial justice.

By turning the march into a commemoration of civil rights activists who had been murdered, the Big Six made the march even more radical than it was.

Now, it would not only demand the creation of jobs for everyone and the destruction of segregation everywhere. It would also demonstrate that the deaths of civil rights martyrs were not in vain, that violent white supremacists could never stop the movement, and that the Black masses would continue to rise up and march on to victory.

Medgar Evers's spirit of resistance lived on.

PART TWO
MAPPING THE MARCH

The centennial of the 1863 Emancipation Proclamation gave a sense of urgency to the demand for civil rights.

Cleveland Robinson, head of the administrative committee, at the march's headquarters in Harlem

6

VISUALIZING THE DAY

The banner was up! There was no mistaking the four-story stucco building on West 130th Street in Harlem. The hand-painted sign, draped across the front, identified it in bold and colorful print: "National Headquarters/March on Washington for Jobs & Freedom/Wed. Aug. 28th."

Martin Luther King, Jr., smiled. Yep! He was at the right place.

Walking through the entranceway, he spotted a small sign pointing visitors to the reception area on the second floor. King bounded up the creaky steps and saw a room full of organized chaos. Phones rang nonstop, desks were stacked high with flyers, and envelopes were strewn on the floor. Volunteers and staffers talked over one another and shouted up and down the steps.

"Where is this young lady who handles the phone?" King said, loud enough for everyone in the room to hear. It wasn't clear whether he was irritated or simply curious.

Patricia Worthy looked up.

She was on summer break from Brooklyn College, with plans to go to law school, and Rustin had hired her to be the office receptionist. Her main job was to answer a ten-line phone that rang day and night, with calls from reporters, politicians, celebrities, everyday people, and the Big Six.

"I want to meet this young lady," King demanded. "She has put me on hold twice, and hung up on me once, and I want to know who she is."

Worthy was horrified. She'd hung up on the most important leader in the civil rights movement!

After she identified herself, King stood silent. Then, he beamed his big smile, walked over to her desk, and gave her a friendly hug. He understood the intense pressure she faced every day.

Breathing a sigh of relief, Worthy returned to her phone. As always, it was flashing.

On the third floor, twenty-two-year-old Rachelle Horowitz filed another 3x5 card with information about a bus, the number of passengers, and the time and location of departure. With each passing hour, the number of cards grew at a pace she'd not predicted.

Like her close friend Tom Kahn, Horowitz was a young socialist who had worked with Rustin on earlier protests. And now she was responsible for organizing all the buses and trains heading to and from the march.

When Rustin had appointed her transportation director, Horowitz was stunned. "How could I possibly do that?" she asked. "I can't drive . . . and also I'm dyslexic about directions!"

"You are *compulsive*," Rustin replied, "and what I want is somebody doing this who will not lose the name of anybody who wants to go to this march, and who needs a bus."

Horowitz answered transportation calls from all over the country. Her friend Norman Hill—who had worked on the first march proposal for Randolph—was rounding up recruits at labor unions and churches in states far and near, and many of them needed advice for getting to and from the march.

Horowitz also made time for everyday Harlem residents who just walked in from the street, hoping to find a way to Washington. If she couldn't find a way, no one could.

Joyce Ladner, a SNCC worker, was out of the office, probably at a church in Long Island or Brooklyn, sharing news about the march and asking for donations to help transport marchers from the South.

Joyce and her sister Dorie were SNCC workers from Mississippi, and both had protested and organized with Medgar Evers. On the night Evers was murdered, Joyce received a call from Ruby Doris Robinson, one of SNCC's main administrators.

"Joyce, Medgar has been killed," Robinson said.

The young activist broke down in tears. "Oh, my God!" she cried. "I've got to go home. I've got to get back to Jackson." At the time, she was representing SNCC at a student conference in Lake Forest, Illinois.

"No," Robinson gently replied. "You need to go to [New York City] and work on the March on Washington."

"But I've known Medgar since I was fourteen," Joyce protested.

*Joyce Ladner in bib overalls,
which SNCC workers fondly
called "freedom uniforms"*

Robinson was insistent. "I want you to get an airline ticket and go to New York City for the rest of the summer to work on the March on Washington," she said. "*This is what Medgar would have wanted you to do.*"

However much it hurt to miss the funeral, Ladner agreed.

Inspired by Evers's courage and dedication, she worked six days a week, raising as much money for the march as possible, often by selling the hundreds of buttons she carried wherever she went. The official march buttons—which showed a white hand and a black hand clasped together—cost twenty-five cents each.

Joyce loved her job, and she was good at it. "Every time Joyce went out to raise money, she came back with enough to rent another bus," Horowitz said.

THREE EARLIER PROTESTS IN WASHINGTON

Bayard Rustin, Tom Kahn, and Rachelle Horowitz had worked together on three earlier protests in Washington: the 1957 Prayer Pilgrimage to Washington and the 1958 and 1959 Youth Marches for Integrated Schools. All three protests called for the speedy implementation of *Brown v. Board of Education of Topeka*, the 1954 US Supreme Court ruling that racial segregation in public schools was unconstitutional. Rustin and his staff drew from their experiences with these three protests when organizing the 1963 march.

Bayard Rustin was in the first-floor office, just behind the staircase. He fretted over the long to-do list on his yellow notepad. The list of tasks changed at lightning speed, and Rustin relied on Tom Kahn, his personal secretary, to help keep track of all the dizzying details.

No detail was too small, and no plan was too basic, to escape Rustin's attention. "If you want to organize anything," he said, "assume that everybody is absolutely stupid. And assume yourself that you're stupid."

Rustin also led the staff meetings at the end of each workday.

Visualize the day of the march, he instructed the staff. *Where will the buses park? Should we greet people at the train station? What should we feed everyone? How many water fountains can we find? What if people get sick? What's the best sound system? And where will everyone go to the bathroom?*

"Toilets were a major concern," John Lewis remembered. "I will never forget Bayard proclaiming, in that rich British accent of his: "Now we *cawn't* have any disorganized *pissing* in Washington."

Sixteen-hour workdays and meals in the office were normal. Sometimes staff members slept at the headquarters, too busy or too tired to make the trek home. Rachelle Horowitz usually went back to her

Rustin and Randolph meet the press at march headquarters.

Bill Mauldin's cartoon of demonstrators marching toward a powder keg reflected public anxiety about the coming protest. (Chicago Sun Times, August 24, 1963)

one-bedroom apartment in the Chelsea neighborhood of Manhattan. Joyce and Dorie Ladner stayed there, too, sleeping on the fold-out sofa.

To Joyce's chagrin, when she arrived back at the apartment, Bob Dylan, a famous folk singer, would sometimes be on the sofa, strumming his guitar and writing a new song. "I wanted to go to sleep, and he would sit there until midnight . . . entertaining Dorie," Joyce recalled.

As the march staff and hundreds of volunteers fell asleep, Rustin obsessed over one major question—*What else can I do to make sure the march is peaceful?*

Meeting all the marchers' needs was one way to make sure that sparks didn't fly, but Rustin still worried about the dire prediction of countless critics—*The march will explode in violence!* As Representative James Haley of Florida put it rather glumly, the march "could be the spark which could touch off an ugly, blood-letting riot, accompanied perhaps by killings."

American Nazi leader George Rockwell, foreground, hated to hear people singing "We Shall Overcome."

7

KENNEDY CAVES

"We will have at least 10,000 white men to stand against the Negroes in Washington," shouted George Lincoln Rockwell, the founder of the American Nazi Party. "If they march, they will have to march over us!"

Speaking to a small crowd in Culpepper, Virginia, Rockwell announced that he was beginning a tour across the state. His plan was to recruit a "white army" to "oppose the Black terrorists" at the upcoming march.

The Nazi leader and his supporters had already distributed thousands of racist pamphlets that warned of a coming "NIGGER REVOLUTON."

"When such an unspeakable, vast, storming ocean of half-ape, African savages—300,000 of them—marches on your Capitol, White Man, you will be WHIPPED!" the pamphlet read.

To avoid the whipping, the American Nazis hoped to put "ONE HUNDRED THOUSAND GRIM-JAWED WHITE MEN SQUARE IN THE PATH OF THAT BLACK SWARM."

On July 11, Julius Hobson, a march staffer based in Washington, DC, reported on Rockwell's plan at an all-important meeting at the Metropolitan Police Department.

The purpose of the meeting—which was attended by Police Chief Robert Murray, Arthur Caldwell of the Justice Department, and

Bayard Rustin, among others—was to exchange information and ideas about security for the march.

Rustin took the occasion to explain that violence at civil rights protests was usually "caused by unorganized or unauthorized whites opposing the demonstration." Exhibit A—George Rockwell and his fellow Nazis. But Rustin also noted that "quite brutal police methods" were another common cause. "If these factors can be controlled or avoided, there is no reason to anticipate violence," he said.

Still, everyone who was present, Rustin included, wanted to plan for it just in case.

THE FIRST AMENDMENT TO THE US CONSTITUTION

"Congress shall make no law respecting an establishment of religion, or prohibiting the free exercise thereof; or abridging the freedom of speech, or of the press; *or the right of the people peaceably to assemble, and to petition the government for a redress of grievances.*"

To his chagrin, Rustin quickly learned that some of his plans posed significant logistical problems. When he said the march would include a demonstration at the White House, followed by a march down Pennsylvania Avenue, a deputy police chief raised a red flag.

"How are you going to get a hundred thousand [marchers near] the White House?" he asked. "That street cannot accommodate more than a few thousand."

Rustin didn't have an answer.

Then, when he conveyed that religious groups hoped to enlist "in excess of 2,000 Protestant, Jewish and Catholic ministers [to] surround the Capitol in prayer during the day," another deputy police chief weighed in.

It's illegal to protest on Capitol grounds, he said. Plus, the Capitol was outside the jurisdiction controlled by the Metropolitan Police Department, having its own security force.

Rustin wasn't sure how to answer this, either.

But he did have a definite opinion on another major issue—police dogs. *No dogs!* Rustin demanded. Images of German shepherds attacking the students of Birmingham were still fresh in his mind, and he believed that police dogs might provoke the marchers.

Snorting at the demand, Police Chief Murray replied that "there would be no dogs assuming there was no trouble."

Assuming there was no trouble?

Back at headquarters, Rustin called William Johnson, a founding member of the Guardians Association, an organization of Black police officers in the New York Police Department. Johnson was an esteemed officer, and his NYPD contacts ran deep.

Rustin poured out his frustration, telling Johnson he did *not* want armed white police officers inside the crowd of mostly Black marchers on August 28. The mix would be volatile, he said.

Instead, he wanted the Guardians to volunteer as marshals who would be responsible for maintaining order and keeping peace. *But no guns and no clubs*, Rustin emphasized. The Guardians would be a nonviolent force. *Oh, and you won't have the power to arrest anyone, either.*

Johnson believed in the march, and he agreed to enlist his fellow Guardians.

The Guardians were given extensive education and guidance. Rustin held some training sessions in the backyard at headquarters.

"Your job is to see that 100,000 persons behave," he told the Guardians, using the most authoritative voice he could muster.

One of the sessions focused on the practice of nonviolent encircle-ment. This called for the Guardians to surround a troublemaker, link arms with one another, and use peaceful language to de-escalate the situation.

"Use every manner of persuasion," Rustin advised. And if that didn't work, the Guardians should escort the troublemaker to DC police offi-cers patrolling the perimeter of the march.

Rustin schooled the Guardian volunteers in nonviolent thought and practice.

For the Guardians, the training was like learning another language; they were accustomed to using threatening words, pulling their guns, and swinging their clubs. But like William Johnson and their demand-ing teacher, the officers believed in the march.

On July 17, President Kennedy held a news conference from the State Department auditorium. He'd just been sailing on the *Honey Fitz*, the White House yacht, and he appeared to be in a good mood. As usual, most of the questions dealt with foreign affairs, but one reporter asked about civil rights protests and the march.

"Do you find that the demonstrations which are taking place are a handicap to you, specifically the Washington march in August?"

"No," Kennedy replied. "We want citizens to come to Washington if they feel that they're not having their rights expressed."

The president said that march organizers were cooperating with "the police," and he even praised the march as a "peaceful assembly calling for a redress of grievances." The march would be in "the great tradition" of "responsible and peaceful" protests.

"I'll look forward to being here," he added. "I'm sure members of Congress will be here."

Kennedy didn't mention his earlier resistance to the march, but it was clear to Rustin and the Big Six that the president had caved, no doubt because he understood that the march was moving full steam ahead, with or without him.

Nor did the president tell the media that his administration was already working behind the scenes to ensure that the march was peaceful. Kennedy's team cooperated with Rustin because they *needed* the march to be a peaceful assembly. A violent eruption, after all, would probably not only defeat the civil rights bill but also sink Kennedy's chances for reelection.

In the days ahead, Rustin would take full advantage of the government's vast resources, including its planning abilities, but neither he nor the Big Six would surrender any control over final decisions. They would not be co-opted.

This was *their* march, and it would stay that way.

Sales of the official button helped
to raise money for the march.

8

MALCOLM X SPEAKS OUT

"Oh, Bayard," said Rachelle Horowitz. "You're turning it into a circus!"

Rustin had just announced dramatic changes to the march.

Circling the Capitol? *Gone.*

Demonstrating at the White House? *Gone.*

Marching down Pennsylvania Avenue? *Gone.*

The reasons behind the changes weren't entirely clear. Perhaps Rustin had heeded the police department's warning that Pennsylvania Avenue, especially in front of the White House, was too small for one hundred thousand marchers, and that a protest on Capitol grounds would be illegal. Perhaps he'd wanted to streamline the march and take away opportunities for things to go wrong in too many places.

Or perhaps he'd compromised with leaders who didn't want Congress and the White House to feel intimidated. Horowitz believed that the Kennedy administration played a role in cutting the demonstrations at the Capitol and the White House.

"The White House absolutely didn't want that to happen," she said later. "And they were able to convince people not to do it."

Whatever the case might have been, Rustin disagreed with the sense that the march had lost its radical edge.

"What you have to understand is that the march will succeed if it gets 100,000 people—or 150,000 or 200,000 or more—to show up in Washington," he argued. "It will be the biggest rally in history. It will show the Black community united as never before—united also with whites from labor and the churches, from all over the country."

For Rustin, the *power* of the march rested in its numbers and coalitions. If marchers didn't protest at the White House, that was okay; location didn't necessarily show power. And if sit-ins were nixed, that was also okay. Militant civil disobedience, even if carried out by several thousand, would demonstrate power, but it would never match the enormous power of a massive march and rally.

Turning out 250,000 people, from all walks of life, for a socialist-inspired march for jobs and freedom to be broadcast across the globe . . . now *that* was powerful and radical!

Nevertheless, to bolster his case, Rustin presented his new plan—a march from the Washington Monument to the Lincoln Memorial, followed by a rally at the Memorial—as an innovative, and revolutionary, way to lobby political leaders.

"The March on Washington projects a new concept of lobbying," Rustin explained in an organizing manual written under his direction. Yes, march leaders would visit with President Kennedy and congressional leaders.

"But in keeping with this new—and more profound—concept of lobbying, our 100,000 marchers will not go to Capitol Hill, nor to the White House.

THE RADICAL MARCH?

On July 20, Rustin and his staff released an eight-page informational booklet that listed the purpose and demands of the march. As you read these, call to mind their historical context. In 1963, the federal government was known for its "go slow" approach to civil rights; racial discrimination and violence against

Black people were pervasive, especially in the South; and Black people suffered from unemployment, underemployment, bias in hiring and firing practices, and a lack of rights in their workplace. Given this context, do you think that the march's purpose and demands were *radical*? Did they seek to *uproot* racial and economic inequality and to *supplant* it with policies and practices that would lead to liberty and justice for all? Or would you use a word other than "radical" to describe the purpose and demands?

What is the purpose of the March?

The purpose of the March is, by a massive, peaceful, and democratic demonstration in the nation's capital, to provide evidence of the need for the Federal Government to take effective and immediate action to deal with the national crisis of civil rights and jobs that all of us, Negro and white, are facing.

What are the demands of the March?

I   The Civil Rights demands include:

Passage by the Congress of effective and meaningful civil rights legislation in the present session, without filibuster.

Immediate desegregation of the nation's schools.

An end to police brutality directed against citizens using their constitutional right of peaceful demonstration.

II   The Job demands include:

A massive Federal Public Works Program to provide jobs for all the unemployed, and Federal legislation to promote an expanding economy.

A Federal Fair Employment Practices Act to bar job discrimination by Federal, State, and Municipal governments, and by private employers, contractors, employment agencies and trade unions.

Broadening of the Federal Fair Labor Standards Act to include the uncovered areas of employment where Negroes and other minorities work at slave wages; and the establishment of a national minimum wage of not less than $2.00 per hour.

A short list of demands appeared in the first organizing manual for the march.

"Instead, we have invited every single Congressman and Senator to *come to us*—to hear our demands for jobs and freedom, NOW . . .

"Our demonstration—the largest and most significant in the history of Washington—will bear eloquent witness that we do not come to beg or plead for rights denied for centuries."

As Rustin saw it, the March on Washington would turn the traditional practice of lobbying upside down.

The old way required individuals to trek up Capitol Hill; the new way called for congressional members to come down from the Hill and meet with the people on a level playing field.

The old way expected one person or a few people to chat with a member of Congress behind closed doors; the new way arranged for members to be surrounded by masses of people in broad daylight.

The old way assumed that people would ask or plead for new laws; the new way urged people to *demand* new laws.

The old way counseled people to be patient while a bill made its way through Congress; the new way demanded new laws *now!*

With this "new—and more profound—concept of lobbying," the march would be "a people's revolution," as Randolph put it.

On August 4, Randolph held a news conference to announce the recent changes.

He also revealed that the Big Six had invited four white men to join the leadership team: Walter Reuther of the United Auto Workers, Reverend Eugene Carson Blake of the National Council of Churches, Rabbi Joachim Prinz of the American Jewish Congress, and Mathew Ahmann of the National Catholic Conference for Interracial Justice. The all-Black Big Six was now the interracial Big Ten.

Randolph also reported that the number of marchers was "much larger than expected." What the march director *didn't* say was that organizers worried that white marchers would outnumber Black marchers—that the "people's revolution" would appear to be a mostly white movement.

At march headquarters, Cleveland Robinson, the chair of the administrative committee, had noticed that Black churches and organizations were slow in signing up for the march. "And time is running out," he warned. Martin Luther King, Jr., was so concerned that he wrote about the problem in a blistering newspaper column.

"Up to this time, the crusade for Negro rights has been sadly lacking in an awareness, by Negroes themselves, of the persuasive power of numbers," King wrote.

"The record on public mass meetings and demonstrations has been . . . bad . . . Mass meetings that should have drawn 2,500 have had 300. Outdoor gatherings where 50,000 should have massed, have had to settle for 16,000."

King offered a recent, and sensitive, example.

"The Medgar Evers assassination was a shot in the back to every Negro in the United States. A silent, powerful demonstration of how they felt would have been to flock to Jackson, Miss., for the funeral. Thousands were present, but tens of thousands should have overflowed every street in the city."

Trying to *radicalize* his Black readers, King delivered a forceful message: Let's break from our disappointing past *now*, and let's march in record numbers on August 28!

WHY DID THE BIG SIX ADD FOUR WHITE MEN?

Why did the Big Six agree to become the Big Ten? Was it because they wanted to broaden the coalition so that it represented white people who would be marching? Because they wanted to use the four leaders to attract marchers from their large organizations (labor unions and churches)? Or because they were running out of money and needed funds that the four white men could help provide? And if the Big Six believed in racial equality, why did they not add *six* white people so that the new group would be equally divided between Black men and white men?

To no one's surprise, Malcolm X spoke out about changes to the march and concerns about the number of Black marchers.

On August 10, Malcolm stood tall on the speaker's platform at the corner of Lenox Avenue and 115th Street in Harlem. He'd organized this "unity meeting" for everyone involved in the Black freedom movement.

Malcolm X told his Harlem supporters that the march organizers had lost control of their own march.

Although he'd invited the Big Six, none of them showed up. Perhaps they suspected that Malcolm would use the rally to criticize the upcoming march. And sure enough, Malcolm charged that the march was now under the control of President Kennedy.

When Kennedy "found out he couldn't stop it, he joined it; and when he joins you, you're not going in the same direction you started in," Malcolm declared.

The crowd of 3,000 laughed. They, too, believed that the president was making the march serve his one and only purpose—passage of a weak civil rights bill.

Later, after learning about concerns over the number of Black marchers, Malcolm added: "The march is a farce—a performance managed by the government and filled by whites.

"There will be more whites than so-called Negroes in the march, and we [in the Nation of Islam] don't participate in anything that whites are in.

"I'll be in Washington that day, but I won't even go there as an observer."

Malcolm's comments about the Kennedy administration weren't altogether accurate.

It was true that the administration was working behind the scenes to ensure that the march was orderly and pro-Kennedy. Within the Big Ten, union leader Walter Reuther—a Kennedy friend and confidant—helped ensure that the march's message and tactics would be favorable toward Kennedy.

It was also true that the Catholic Kennedys were strongly urging Catholic leaders to turn out as many parishioners as possible, and that at the time the majority of Catholics in the US were white people.

But, unknown to Malcolm, there was one powerful person in the Kennedy administration who considered the march a *radical* threat to national security.

His top-secret plan to sabotage the march was about to go public.

FBI Director J. Edgar Hoover, left, and his boss, Attorney
General Robert Kennedy, opposed the march.

9

THE FBI ATTACKS

J. Edgar Hoover saw red.

The FBI director believed that the civil rights movement was controlled by communists plotting to overthrow the US government, and now that the March on Washington planning was in full swing, he was determined to stop it.

Reviewing his secret files, he settled on a target.

On August 1, Associated Press reporter Junius Griffin showed up at march headquarters and asked for an interview with Bayard Rustin. Although the deputy director was swamped with work, he agreed to talk.

Unknown to Rustin, Griffin was armed with information that J. Edgar Hoover had initially supplied to Strom Thurmond, the segregationist senator from South Carolina.

Thurmond and Hoover were allies. Both saw the civil rights movement as communist inspired, and both wanted to undermine the radical march. Hoover had provided Thurmond with FBI files about Rustin, knowing that the senator would leak them to the press. And that's what happened.

With the FBI files as his source, Griffin asked Rustin about his past arrests, including his 1953 arrest on sex charges. The question about 1953 took Rustin by surprise, and he stumbled for an answer.

"I was sentenced to 60 days, but I was a very young man at the time, and I do not care to elaborate on it," he said. "This might cost me my job. I am going to bring it up at our next meeting and let the civil rights leaders decide if this part of my background will affect the cause."

Griffin also inquired about Rustin's past associations with communists. Rustin denied that he, or any other march organizer, was a communist.

The interview rattled Rustin, and he immediately contacted Randolph. True to form, the veteran labor leader refused to panic. He was used to bare-knuckled political battles, and this one, while dangerous, seemed winnable. Two days later, reporters asked Randolph whether Rustin would resign or be fired.

"No," Randolph replied, "Mr. Rustin is Mr. March-on-Washington himself."

The answer infuriated Senator Thurmond.

"If Rustin is Mr. March-on-Washington himself, they ought to call off the whole thing," Thurmond huffed. "It is terrible for a man with such a record to be conducting the demonstration and in such close cooperation with officials of the Kennedy administration."

On August 13—fifteen days from March Day—the senator ramped up his public attack on Rustin.

Standing in the Senate well, Thurmond used information from FBI files to criticize Rustin's arrest for refusing military service in World War II, his many arrests for civil disobedience, his past membership in the Young Communist League, his attendance at a Communist Party convention, and his failure to denounce "Communist ideological dogma."

Thurmond also put newspaper articles about Rustin's 1953 arrest into the *Congressional Record*—the government's published record of congressional debates and proceedings. Commenting on the articles, Thurmond said that Rustin "was arrested for vagrancy and lewdness,"

Ruskin Article Goes In Record

Related Stories on Page 6

By FRANK VAN DER LINDEN
Chief of Banner's
Washington Bureau

Washington — Sen. Strom Thurmond, D-S.C., has placed in the Congressional Record information that Bayard Rustin, deputy director of the Aug. 28 civil rights March on Washington, is a former Communist who served jail terms for sex perversion and violating the draft law.

Thurmond put into the record — where it is privileged information, free from libel suits — a Washington Post article which he called a "whitewash" of Rustin.

The Post story said the New York Negro was a former member of the Young Communist League and attended the Communist convention in 1956 in New York as an "observer."

'Fuzzy View'

"It gives a fuzzy explanation that he quit the Young Communist League because he was non-violent and because the league accepted racial segregation in the armed forces after Hitler attacked Russia," Thurmond told the Senate.

However, the senator said,

(Turn to Page 6, Column 5)

BAYARD RUSTIN
—Pasadena Police Department Photo.

Rustin's name is misspelled in this Nashville Banner *article on his 1953 arrest.*

and was guilty of "sex perversion." In effect, the senator outed Rustin as a gay man, and a convicted one at that, to an entire nation.

The national news media latched onto Thurmond's remarks. A United Press International article even accurately reported that the senator inserted "FBI records" into the *Congressional Record*.

The media frenzy was too significant to ignore or dismiss, and the Big Ten decided to hold an emergency meeting to craft a response. The big question before the meeting was, *How will Roy Wilkins respond?* The NAACP leader, after all, had strongly warned that opponents would use Rustin's past to target the march.

At the meeting, the Big Ten were agitated, to say the least. Wilkins was livid—*but only at Thurmond!* The NAACP leader said that the Big Ten should never allow the senator to dictate their actions. Instead, they should rally to Rustin's side and defend him publicly.

Right after the meeting, Martin Luther King, Jr., did exactly that, praising Rustin's "abilities and achievements." Randolph did the same in a statement he issued to the press.

"I am sure I speak for the combined Negro leadership in voicing my complete confidence in Bayard Rustin's character, integrity, and extraordinary ability," Randolph stated.

"Twenty-two arrests in the fight for civil rights attest, in my mind, to Mr. Rustin's dedication to high human ideals."

Randolph even referred to the 1953 arrest.

"That Mr. Rustin was on one occasion arrested in another connection has long been a matter of public record, and not an object of concealment. There are those who contend that this incident, which took place many years ago, voids or overwhelms Mr. Rustin's ongoing contribution to the struggle for human rights. I hold otherwise."

South Carolina senator Strom
Thurmond failed in his attempt to
undermine the march by attacking
Rustin's moral character.

Then, taking direct aim at Thurmond and Hoover, Randolph concluded: "I am dismayed that there are men in this country who, wrapping themselves in the mantle of Christian morality, would mutilate the
most elementary conceptions of human decency, privacy, and humility
in order to persecute other men. We are not fooled, however, into be-
lieving that these men are interested in Mr. Rustin. They seek only to
discredit the movement."

"And that was that," Rustin assistant Tom Kahn recalled. "It was like a
boil being lanced."

As the Thurmond crisis faded, a relieved Rustin went back to work.
But the feeling of relief was short-lived. Another crisis, this one from
within the team of organizers, was about to erupt.

*Marchers—mostly women—from several states in 1954
gathered in front of the White House to protest a recent
quadruple lynching in Georgia.*

10

THE WOMEN DEMAND

Just a week to go.

Cleveland Robinson, the chair of the administrative committee, was feeling intense pressure to wrap up all the details. Today's meeting, with the Big Ten in attendance, would review changes to the Lincoln Memorial program.

Anna Arnold Hedgeman—the only woman on the committee—was looking forward to this moment, and she immediately scanned the list of speakers.

She could barely contain her anger.

Not one woman was on the list.

Hedgeman had fought hard to bring women into the march. Just after joining the committee, she'd advocated for Dorothy Height, the leader of the National Council of Negro Women, to become an official leader of the march, on equal par with A. Philip Randolph and other civil rights leaders. But the men ignored her idea.

Then, Hedgeman and Height joined forces and lobbied Bayard Rustin to add women to the Lincoln Memorial program.

"Women are included," Rustin replied. "Every group has women in it."

Height and Hedgeman scoffed at that response and continued their fight, pointing out that "women were the backbone of the movement."

"We knew, firsthand, that most of the civil rights movement audiences were largely comprised of women, children, and youth," Height said. Hedgeman also knew that many of the people she was recruiting—she worked full-time for the National Council of Churches—were women activists in their local communities.

Still, the men refused to budge. They claimed that the Big Ten spoke for women, that the program was already too long, and that it would be difficult to select one woman "without causing serious problems vis-à-vis other women and women's groups."

Hedgeman fought hard to include a woman speaker in the Lincoln Memorial program on March Day.

Plus, they said, "We have Mahalia Jackson."

Hedgeman and Height were pleased that the gospel singer was scheduled for the official program. "But she is not speaking," they protested. "She's not speaking on behalf of women, or on behalf of civil rights. She's singing."

The men shrugged their shoulders.

"I've never seen a more immovable force," Height said later. "We could not get women's participation taken seriously."

THE YOUNG FEMINIST

In May 1941, Anna Arnold Hedgeman, then the executive secretary of the Brooklyn YWCA, spoke with Black women undergraduates at Hampton Institute in Virginia. In her lecture, Hedgeman warned that although "all women have serious employment problems, Negro women carry the additional handicap of colored with its attendant discrimination with regard to training, apprentice opportunities, and job opportunities." Hedgeman added that Black women must be "better prepared" than any other worker if they are to succeed in their chosen professions. The *Atlanta Daily World*, in its front-page article about the lecture, described Hedgeman as "the young feminist."

Now, at the meeting to review the Lincoln Memorial program, Hedgeman seethed. Politely but firmly, she pushed yet again for adding a woman speaker.

The men folded their arms.

But Hedgeman didn't relent.

The men sat silent.

Hedgeman stared at them.

The tense standoff continued until someone finally proposed a compromise. *What if Randolph says a few words about the contributions of women to the civil rights movement? He could acknowledge a group of leading women activists, and after he speaks, they could stand for a round of applause.*

Even the most militant member of the Big Six—John Lewis of SNCC—seemed fine with the proposal, but for Hedgeman, it was little better than nothing. As usual, she resolved to fight on. Shortly after the meeting, the radical feminist put her protest in writing, in a forceful letter she sent to the Big Ten.

Several days before the march, the administrative committee held its last meeting. The room buzzed with excitement as the committee reviewed the final checklist.

How many will be there? everyone wondered. Committee chair Robinson predicted two hundred thousand—double the number of their earliest goal.

As the meeting wound down, Hedgeman asked for permission to speak. She looked serious, and the room grew quiet. The Big Ten must have known what was coming. Each had received her letter of protest, and none had responded. With her letter in hand, Hedgeman rose from her chair and began reading.

"In light of the role of Negro women in the struggle for freedom and especially in light of the extra burden they have carried because of the castration of our Negro man in this culture, it is incredible that no woman should appear as a speaker at the historic March on Washington Meeting at the Lincoln Memorial."

The men sat silently; no one dared to interrupt.

"Since the 'Big Six' have not given women the quality of participation which they have earned through the years," Hedgeman continued, "I would like to suggest the following:

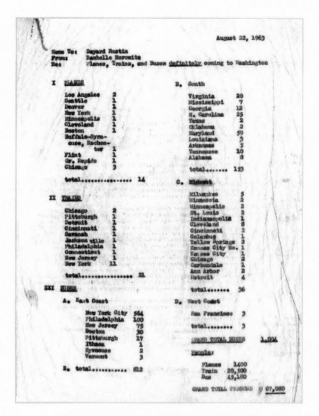

Horowitz's transportation memorandum shows a number far less than the two hundred thousand marchers that Cleveland Robinson predicted.

"That a Negro woman make a brief statement and present the other Heroines just as you have suggested the Chairman [Randolph] might do." Hedgeman also recommended two possible candidates to serve as presenter—Myrlie Evers and Diane Nash.

Taking her seat, Hedgeman waited for the usual response.

Roy Wilkins—whose NAACP had more women members than all the other organizations combined—spoke first.

"No one can quarrel with that statement," he said. "I think the case is made."

Hedgeman was shocked. She'd finally moved the mountain of male resistance.

WHY DID RANDOLPH INVITE ANNA ARNOLD HEDGEMAN?

Randolph invited Hedgeman to serve on the administrative committee in early 1963. He turned to her because she was a highly accomplished veteran in the fight for economic justice for Black people. The two had worked together in the March on Washington Movement in the early 1940s. Three years later, Randolph recruited Hedgeman to become executive director of the National Council for a Permanent Fair Employment Practices Committee. In this role, she lobbied Congress to fund a permanent government committee that would work to eliminate discrimination in employment.

Following Hedgeman's suggestion, the committee elected to invite Myrlie Evers to lead a "Tribute to Negro Women, Fighters for Freedom."

The brief testimonial would recognize the outstanding work of Evers and five other women in particular: Rosa Parks, who had sparked the Montgomery bus boycott; Daisy Bates, who had led the fight to desegregate schools in Little Rock, Arkansas; Diane Nash, who had headed the Nashville student movement and participated in the Freedom Rides; Prince Lee, the widow of murdered SNCC helper Herbert Lee; and Gloria Richardson, the militant leader of the still-raging desegregation protests in Cambridge, Maryland. The women would stand for the tribute, but they would not have a chance to speak. The committee also decided that the honorees, along with the wives of the civil rights leaders, would lead one of two lines of marchers. The Big Ten would lead one up Constitution Avenue, and the women would lead the other up Independence Avenue. The two lines would converge at the Lincoln Memorial.

Finally, the committee agreed to reserve prominent seats near the speaker's podium for other Black women leaders, including Dorothy Height. These veteran activists would sit with the honorees and the wives of the civil rights leaders.

Hedgeman appreciated the changes, but she was still bothered. After all, not one woman would give a major speech, and women were relegated to what she knew would be the smaller line of a segregated march.

Making matters worse, A. Philip Randolph had agreed to speak at the all-male National Press Club a few days before the march.

The club, which hosted speeches by newsmakers, excluded women as members. If women journalists reported on a club event, they were required to stand in the balcony—and be quiet.

When white reporter Elsie Carper learned that Randolph would be speaking at the exclusive club, she fumed.

"It is ludicrous and at the same time distressing that a group fighting for civil rights has chosen a private and segregated male-only club for its first press appearance in Washington . . . The balcony, as well as the back of the bus, should have special meaning to civil rights leaders."

Pauli Murray, a radical Black activist for civil rights and women's rights, had a similar reaction, and in a letter to Randolph, she criticized his decision, saying it "can only be construed to mean that you are only concerned with the rights of Negro men only and care little for the rights of all people."

Murray also delivered a thinly veiled threat. "Frankly," she wrote, "if I were a newspaper woman and you persisted in carrying out this invitation, I would picket you and question your sincerity about human rights."

Randolph tried to defend himself.

Pauli Murray lashes out at back row role

After the march, Pauli Murray continued to criticize A. Philip Randolph and others for excluding women from prominent roles.

WASHINGTON — Miss Pauli Murray, attorney, and a member of the Committee on Civil and Political Rights of the President's Commission of the Status of Women" charged male civil rights leaders with prejudice, here, Thursday.

Miss Murray, who spoke at the annual convention of the National Council of Women, charged that the men are assigning their women to "secondary, ornamental" roles in the civil rights movement.

"It was bitterly humiliating for women on Aug. 28 to see themselves accorded little more than token recognition in the historic March on Washington." Miss Murray said.

"Not a single woman was invited to make one of the major speeches or to be part of the delegation of leaders who went to the White House," she said.

THEIR OMISSION was "deliberate," she added, singling out A. Philip Randolph, chief of tre March leaders, for extra criticism.

Two days before the March, she said, Mr. Randolph, chief of the March Press Club "in the face of strong protest by organized newspaperwomen at the club. The club sends women reporters who cover its luncheon to the balcony.

"Mr. Randolph apparently saw no relationship between being sent to the balcony and being sent to the back of the bus."

THIS WAS not an isolated incident Miss Murray said. "Women who have been active in local branches of the NAACP have observed the efforts of men to push them out of positions of leadership."

Miss Murray also challenged recent statements by James Meredith that women and children should not be used "in certain exposed roles in our fight."

"All colored Americans are born involved in the civil rights fight and exposed to its dangers" she said.

"IRONICALLY ENOUGH, the very presence of women and children in the demonstrations has doubtless minimized the violence and aroused the sympathies of the American public.

"Bearing in mind that everything possible must be done to encourage colored males to develop their highest educational potential and to accept their family responsibilities and feel secure in colored women have no alternative but to insist upon equal opportunities without regard to sex in training, education and employment at every level.

"This may be a matter of sheer survival," Miss Murray said. "And these special needs must be articulated by the civil rights movement so that they are not overlooked."

"It's a hectic time," he said. "I got the invitation and accepted. I heard the club had an all-male policy afterwards."

But Randolph refused to withdraw from the engagement.

"It would be uncivil," he said.

Murray made plans to picket Randolph, but when she sought to enlist others, she discovered that some women didn't want to do anything that might undermine the credibility of the march.

Dropping her plans, Murray had mixed feelings as she packed her bags for the march. She was looking forward to protesting for civil rights, but it pained her that "Negro women were accorded little more than token recognition on the March program."

That just wasn't right.

JANE CROW

In 1947, Pauli Murray coined the term "Jane Crow" to describe Black women's experience of racial discrimination and gender-based discrimination. Historically, "Jim Crow" referred to laws and customs designed to prevent Black people from exercising their constitutional rights. By using "Jane Crow," Murray argued that Black women faced not only Jim Crow but also laws and customs designed to relegate *women* to second-class citizenship.

PART THREE
ON THE WAY

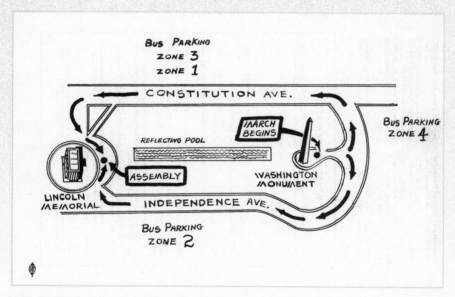

Plans called for women to lead the march down Independence Avenue, one of the two streams of people leading to the Lincoln Memorial on the official program's map.

Surrounded by white onlookers, young Black people leading an anti-segregation protest in Gadsden, Alabama, June 10, 1963

THREE HITCHHIKERS—AND THE STUDENTS LEFT BEHIND

Let's hitchhike!

Frank Thomas's good friends, Robert Avery and James Smith, perked up, but they weren't exactly sure that he was being serious. They were only teenagers, and Washington, DC, was hundreds of miles from Gadsden, Alabama. But the more they talked about going to the march, the more excited they became.

Fifteen-year-old Robert decided not to beat around the bush when asking his mother for permission.

"We're getting ready to go to Washington," he said in a gentle voice. "We're going to be hitchhiking. I need a change of clothes, and whatever money you might have."

His mother already knew about Robert's commitment to civil rights. He and his friends had been active in the local movement for the better part of the summer—picketing businesses, marching through town, and attending rallies. On several occasions, they had been arrested.

Robert's mother also understood that the trio of friends didn't have enough money for bus tickets. Between them, they had ten dollars, sixty-five dollars less than the total price for three roundtrip tickets.

"OK," she replied, "just be careful."

Somehow, Frank and James also snagged permission, and the trio left on Sunday, August 18, hoping to make the 686-mile trek in about a week.

The trip smelled of danger. Gadsden and the surrounding areas were not safe places for Black people demanding their rights. In June, state troopers had wielded nightsticks and electrical cattle prods in a vicious assault on protesters at the Gadsden courthouse. "It was brutal as hell," said a local law officer.

Whites who supported civil rights also faced horror. In April, William Moore, the CORE activist who would be commemorated at the march, had been shot and killed on US Highway 11 just seven miles from Robert's home, during his one-man civil rights march from Tennessee to Mississippi.

The murder of William Moore inspired Frank, James, and Robert as they began their journey to Washington. This historical marker is located in Moore's hometown of Binghamton, New York.

Frank, James, and Robert walked along Highway 11 on their way to Washington. The site of Moore's murder was just up the road, and the three decided to stop there for a moment of reflection.

"Here's this man who gave his life for us," Frank said, "This should encourage us to go on."

The friends also bowed their heads and said a prayer for Moore and his family, and for their own protection. Inspired by Moore's dedication, the trio walked on, hoping for a safe ride.

Sometime after midnight, a white Greyhound bus driver spotted them outside Chattanooga, Tennessee. The worried driver pulled over and asked them why they were on a dark road in the middle of the night.

"Y'all are crazy," he said. "Do you all know where you're at? You need to get on this bus."

The teens hopped aboard, grateful for the comfortable ride to Chattanooga.

Jazz artists were not featured on March Day, but they played an important role in raising funds for the march.

Back on the road after a bit of sleep, the friends tried to attract riders with a handmade sign that read, "Washington or Bust."

A white driver saw the message and slowed down. The trio looked inside the car, waiting for an offer, but the man screamed at them: "*Boom!*"

The friends jumped back from the car, scared to death. They knew that some white people in the area used dynamite to terrorize civil rights activists.

As the man sped away, the trio ditched the sign. From now on, their destination was not "Washington or *Bust.*" It was "Washington or Washington."

Most drivers were welcoming. *Hop in*, they would say. *Where y'all heading?* Everyone would swap stories and share a good laugh.

When a white man in a pickup truck pulled over, the teens squeezed together in the front seat, ready for some friendly banter.

"You boys know it's dangerous out here?" the man asked.

"Yeah," they replied.

"Y'all need to be careful," he warned.

But his tone made it sound like a threat, and the hair stood up on the back of Robert's neck. The creepy man didn't say anything else that was threatening, but Robert breathed a sigh of relief when the ride was over.

Despite the scares, the friends continued to thumb rides. In Lynchburg, Virginia, a friendly Black family on their way to Washington invited them to jump in.

Nestled in their seats, the teens enjoyed the ride through the beautiful back mountains of Virginia. Everything was lush and green, and the sweet smell of wildflowers filled the car.

But then the friends saw something that sent shivers up and down their spines—an effigy, or dummy, of a Black person hanging on a light pole outside a gas station. It looked like a lynching.

The scene served as a gruesome warning to Black people thinking about stopping for gas or a restroom break. It also reminded the teens that they would be marching not only for jobs and freedom, but also for their very lives.

At 3:00 a.m. on Wednesday, August 21, the family dropped off Frank, James, and Robert in a safe spot in downtown Washington. They had arrived!

But now what to do? The friends had thirty-five cents between them, and it was one week until March Day. They approached a nearby police officer for some advice, and he suggested that they check out the local NAACP headquarters.

The office was closed, of course, but a sign on the door listed the

SIGNS AND BANNERS

Two kinds of signs will be carried in the March:

1. *Signs of Identification:* These signs may be made and carried only by groups that fall into one of the following categories:

    a) religious groups
    b) labor unions and bodies
    c) fraternal organizations
    d) sponsoring civil rights organizations and their affiliates.

Groups in these four categories may put signs or streamers of identification on their buses as well. All other groups may identify their bus only with signs or streamers reading MARCH ON WASHINGTON FOR JOBS AND FREEDOM, AUGUST 28, 1963.

2. *Slogans:* All slogans carried in this March will be designed exclusively by the National Committee and will be distributed at the Washington Monument.

FOOD, HEALTH, AND SANITATION FACILITIES

FOOD: We urge all marchers to take 2 box lunches—one for midday, one for supper. These box lunches should be kept simple and balanced. Exclude perishable or spoilable foods—no mayonnaise or salads, for example. We suggest:

    peanut butter and jelly sandwiches
    an apple or other fruit
    a brownie or plain cake
    a soft drink.

HEALTH AND SANITATION: Several government agencies, Church World Service, and local churches have cooperated with the National Committee to provide for your health and comfort. First-aid units and mobile toilets will be available. Cots, blankets, and other rest facilities will be provided. Ample drinking water will be accessible at many points.

A word of advice. You can help relieve pressure on these facilities by taking good care of yourself:

1. Get a good night's sleep the night before.
2. Take advantage of rest facilities en route to Washington.
3. Be kind to your stomach—don't eat or drink the wrong foods in the wrong quantities.

CHILDREN AND OVERNIGHT ACCOMMODATIONS

This is a one day demonstration

The size and scope of this March make it imperative that all participants come in and go out on the same day—August 28th.

You are *strongly advised* not to bring children under 14; children over 14 should be accompanied by a parent or guardian.

Should an emergency or unusual circumstance require your remaining overnight, call the Washington Urban League at REpublic 7-0367.

10

CAPTAINS

Every bus, train, and plane must have a captain. Here are the duties of a captain:

1. He must have an accurate list of the passengers under his charge—including their names and addresses. He must check this list at every discharge and boarding point.

2. He must be sure that each member of his group knows when the bus (train or plane) leaves.

3. En route to Washington, he must read to his passengers the March schedule and regulations presented in this manual.

4. He must make sure that there are first aid supplies on his bus, and pay special attention to this manual's instructions on food and health.

5. Before permitting passengers to leave the bus in Washington, the captain must give each passenger an index card. On this card each passenger should write the parking location and license plate number of the bus, as dictated by the captain.

6. In general, captains are responsible for the welfare and discipline of their groups—on the road and in Washington. Every captain should have this number to call in case of emergency in Washington: REpublic 7-0367.

All local groups must gather their captains together in advance for briefings. Make sure that every captain has read this manual thoroughly and can explain its contents to others. If you have any questions, call or write our office.

MARSHALS

We have our own system of internal marshaling. Some 2,000 trained men stand ready to assist you in maintaining order and comfort during the March.

These marshals will be conspicuously identified. An elaborate communications network will enable them to be in contact with each other and with the Washington police.

Should problems of order or discipline arise, bus captains should call upon a marshal.

11

Organizers sought to exclude children who were fourteen years old and younger, but that didn't stop thousands of young people from attending the march.

name of Walter Fauntroy as the local march coordinator. So the trio found a nearby public phone and inserted one of their three remaining dimes.

The call jolted Fauntroy out of his sleep. *What? Three teens from Alabama? Hitchhikers? Here for the march? No money?*

Fauntroy was aware of the march's guideline regarding young people. An official document titled *Organizing Manual No. 2* read, "You are *strongly advised* not to bring children under 14; children over 14 should be accompanied by a parent or guardian."

The guideline probably struck some as odd if not infuriating. It suggested that the organizers were leaving students behind despite their monumental contributions to the march. It was the Birmingham students, after all, who had fueled the march's beginning. Plus, young people in Birmingham and elsewhere continued to serve as a main source of inspiration for countless adults planning to march.

But now, adult organizers were treating students the same way they treated women, though a bit worse. No students served on any of the march committees, no students would be honored at the march, and no students would speak at the march.

But Fauntroy wasn't about to desert these three teenagers. Their initiative and bravery impressed him, so he arranged for them to spend the night at the YMCA and told them to meet him at march headquarters the following day.

The next morning, Fauntroy hired the teens at three dollars a day to help make protest signs and buttons. A local organization led by Black women, the National Beauty Culturists' League, also learned of the teens' plight and offered to provide them with free room and board.

"Wow!" the trio said. "Girls!"

The boys were thrilled, but when they arrived at the League's headquarters, they discovered that "the youngest was probably 65."

The friends spent most of their time making thousands of signs with the march's official messages: WE MARCH FOR JOBS FOR ALL *NOW!* WE DEMAND EQUAL RIGHTS *NOW!* WE MARCH FOR INTEGRATED SCHOOLS *NOW!* By the end of the first workday, no teenager in the world knew the march's ten demands better than Frank, James, and Robert.

One day before the march, Martin Luther King, Jr., stopped by the office. He had just come from Gadsden, Alabama, where he'd talked about local protests as well as the march.

FAREWELL TO MARCHERS — Dr. Katie E. Wickam, president of the National Beauty Culturists League, Inc. says goodbye to three teenagers who hitch hiked from Gadsden, Ala. to Washington for the freedom march. The League provided lodging and board for the youngsters at its national headquarters here. The youths, from left, are James Smith, Robert Avery and Robert Thomas. Members of the League looking on are, from left, Mrs. Louise Wilson, Mrs. Amelia Hill, Mrs. Serene B. Patterson, Mrs. Gladys Spinner and Mrs. Elizabeth Lee.

The hitchhikers bidding farewell before heading back to Gadsden (Afro-American, September 14, 1963)

The friends couldn't believe it. They had long dreamed of seeing their hero, and here he was, standing right in front of them.

After they exchanged greetings, King turned to Robert.

"I just left your hometown," he said, "and your parents asked me to make sure you're OK."

Robert was shocked. The world's most important civil rights leader was on a mission from his parents! The teen smiled and assured him that all was good.

King thanked the trio for their important work, and then he excused himself.

He had a speech to write.

12

FREEDOM TRAINS

The brakes screeched as the B&O trains pulled into Chicago's Grand Central Station.

It was a little before 3:30 p.m. on Tuesday, August 27, and about sixteen hundred people waited to board two trains bound for the march. The scene was "nothing short of pandemonium," a reporter observed.

Timuel Black, a co-chair of the local march committee, beamed as he stood among the throngs of travelers.

"This overwhelming response is a clear indication of the intensity of the grassroots revolt that is taking place in the Negro community," he declared.

Black, a forty-four-year-old schoolteacher, had spent countless hours recruiting the marchers now jammed together on the train platform. For him, the work was part of a long personal crusade.

As a soldier during World War II, he'd helped liberate the Buchenwald concentration camp where Jewish people and others had been murdered in Hitler's pursuit of racial purity. With the horrific images haunting him as he returned home, he pledged to spend the rest of his life "trying to make where I live, and the bigger world, a place where all people could have peace and justice."

Black's organizing work for the march was another expression of his long fight against white supremacy. It was also part of his desire to build a better life for his family. Accompanying him on the trip were his fifteen-year-old daughter and, yes, his ten-year-old son. Like thousands

Last Call   for ALL Americans to join the . . .

MARCH ON WASHINGTON

★   *FOR JOBS and FREEDOM*   ★

WEDNESDAY, AUGUST 28th, 1963

America faces a crisis . . .

Millions of Negroes are denied freedom . . . .

Millions of citizens, black and white, are unemployed . . . .

The twin evils of discrimination and economic deprivation plague the Nation and rob all people, Negro and White, of dignity and self-respect. As long as black workers are voteless, exploited, ill-housed, denied education and underpaid the fight of the white workers for decent wages and working conditions will fail.

We Are Marching . . .

for freedom

● To demand the passage of effective civil rights legislation in the present session which will guarantee to all:
   decent housing
   access to all accommodations
   immediate desegregation of the Nation's schools
   the right to vote

● An end to police brutality directed against citizens using constitutional right of peaceful demonstration.

● To prevent compromise or filibuster against such legislation

for jobs

   ● To demand a Federal massive works and training program that puts all unemployed workers, black and white, back to work

   ● To demand an FEP Act which bars discrimination by Federal, state and municipal governments, by private employers, by contractors, employment agencies and trade unions

   ● To demand a national minimum wage of not less than $2.00 per hour which covers all workers

Ride the Chicago **FREEDOM TRAIN**

Special rate $27.00 per passenger — round trip

Leaves Chicago late afternoon Tuesday, August 27th / Arrives back in Chicago afternoon Thursday, August 29th

For Further Information:

CHICAGO COMMITTEE

MARCH ON WASHINGTON

FOR JOBS AND FREEDOM

4859 South Wabash Avenue   Chicago 15, Illinois   ●   Phone 624-1810

*An advertisement for the Freedom Train
transporting marchers from Chicago to Washington
(Chicago Daily Defender, August 21, 1963)*

of others, Black had ignored or dismissed the march manual's advice about leaving children fourteen and under at home.

As Black and his children waited for the train doors to open, a white journalist named Studs Terkel strolled through the restless crowd, asking people what the train trip meant to them.

MARCHING!

2500 Jam Station Enroute To March

By LLOYD GENERAL

The scene of Chicago's Grand Central station yesterday afternoon was nothing short of pandemonium. Traffic was snarled for blocks around as thousands of Chicago Negroes and whites converged on the station.

Their destination was Washington where the greatest civil rights rally in the United States history will be held today.

There were some 2500 persons jammed in the station, including prominent Chicago citizens and the lowly and meek.

They had one goal — freedom. And to achieve it, they had chartered two trains of the Baltimore and Ohio railroad, which departed from Chicago shortly after 3 p.m.

Meanwhile Senate Republican Leader Everett M. Dirksen said he will meet leaders of the civil rights march this morning in his capitol office—

and there only.

The Illinois Republican said he told the march leaders their meeting with him would be "in my office, period." Dirksen said he understood there had been a suggestion that the session be held in Vice President Lyndon B. Johnson's office.

A spokesman for Johnson said the Vice President does not plan to participate in the 9:30 A.M. session but will meet the leaders with President Kennedy at the White House at 5 P.M. as announced.

On the day of the march, the Daily Defender *estimated that the train station in Chicago was jammed with "2500 persons" heading to the march the previous afternoon.*

"I hope this train is gonna reach freedom," one Black man said. Another was more specific. "It means an opportunity to earn a living in my country."

On board, Terkel spotted Etta Moten Barnett, a well-known singer and actress. Barnett was the first Black woman to sing in the White House; she'd also starred in the 1942 revival of *Porgy and Bess*, an enormously popular Broadway musical.

With Terkel's microphone in front of her, Barnett summed up her feelings about the march by quietly singing an old religious hymn:

> *This train is bound for glory, this train.*
> *This train is bound for glory, this train.*
> *This train is bound for glory,*
> *And when I get there, I'm gonna tell my story.*

"And this train is bound for Washington," Barnett added, "and I hope these leaders of ours, when they get to the White House, will really tell our story." She was referring to the Big Ten, especially the Black leaders, and their plan to visit President Kennedy on March Day.

Looking at the steel mills outside her window, Barnett explained that "our story" was about the lack of jobs. Yes, there were "some jobs for some people," she said, but there was an urgent need "for all people to have jobs." And not just any jobs, but good ones that paid well.

While Barnett spoke in a gracious tone, other passengers sounded frustrated.

"I've seen so many unfair things happen to my people, unfair things happen to me," an older woman said in a sharp, bitter tone.

"I could never say that America is the land of the free and the home of the brave. It's a land of prejudice, hatred . . . I'm so mad when I think about it."

But she also said that she felt "wonderful," especially about the young people on board. "I have a soft heart for all young people, all youth," she explained. "There's hope in them."

The communal spirit on the train also encouraged her. "If every white man and woman in America would get on this train and see the good fellowship, he'd either have a stroke or he might have a change of heart."

In another part of the train, Muriel Thompson saw fellow passengers who weren't as well dressed as she was. Thompson was sensitive to their difficult economic circumstances—and the financial hardship of the journey. A roundtrip ticket, plus three meals, cost $31.80. Finding that money was a steep challenge for many.

Eager to share from her abundance, Thompson opened a large suitcase full of individually wrapped pieces of chicken that she'd fried the night before. The smell of fresh chicken filled the train car, and stomachs everywhere began to growl and grumble. But they didn't complain long. Thompson soon gave away every piece.

Around this same time, Attorney General Robert Kennedy— the president's younger brother—was at an exclusive dinner party in Georgetown, a swanky and largely white neighborhood in Washington, DC. Ambassador Marietta Tree, the US delegate to the United Nations, was also there. She usually lived in New York City, but she was in Washington for the march.

When Kennedy found that out, he said to her: "So you're down here for that old black fairy's anti-Kennedy demonstration?"

Tree was taken aback by Kennedy's slur about Bayard Rustin's homosexuality. Ever the diplomat, she switched the topic and began talking about Martin Luther King, Jr. But Kennedy made a mean-spirited comment about him, too.

The attorney general was in a surly mood, and there was no doubt that the march was the source of his surliness. Despite his brother's declared support for the march, despite his own cooperation with Rustin, and despite the march leaders' backing of the civil rights bill, the attorney general still saw the march as a massive protest of the Kennedy administration and its civil rights policies.

Robert F. Kennedy addressing protesters at the Department of Justice shortly after the murder of Medgar Evers

Perhaps he was right about that, or at least partly right. While many folks on the way to the march praised the Kennedy brothers, others saw them as major obstructions to Black freedom. For these folks, the brothers were privileged, sheltered, wealthy white people who could never understand the dreams of Black people, let alone their nightmares.

In fact, at this very moment, more than a handful of radical anti-Kennedy activists were picketing Robert Kennedy's Department of Justice.

13

SNCC PICKETS, MALCOLM POKES

While Robert Kennedy attended that dinner party on the eve of the march, about twenty SNCC activists picketed the Department of Justice (DOJ) at 10th and Pennsylvania Avenues.

One of the protest signs read, "The Justice Department Is a White Man." The provocative message suggested that the DOJ was far from a bastion of justice; that just like unlawful white segregationists, it was bigoted toward Black people.

Tonight's protesters were angry especially about the department's recent announcement that it had found no evidence of police brutality in Americus, Georgia, a small city about 135 miles south of Atlanta.

SNCC picketing the Department of Justice on the eve of the march

On August 8, about 250 activists in Americus, many of them Black teenagers, met in a downtown church to discuss racial segregation in their hometown. After the meeting, the group gathered outside a Black-friendly café about a block away from the church. As they sang "We Shall Overcome," police officers fired their guns into the air and told everyone to disperse.

When the group refused to move, officers attacked, swinging their clubs at anyone in their way. They also beat and arrested three SNCC activists, charging them with seditious conspiracy. If convicted, the three would face the death penalty.

The next day, about 175 Black folks demonstrated against the police violence of the prior night. According to local activist John Barnum, the group "walked four blocks in orderly columns of twos, not blocking the sidewalk. The police officers were armed with guns, two-foot clubs, electric cattle prodders, and blackjacks . . . the City Marshal and Police Chief asked them if they had a permit to parade and asked them to disperse. But before any response could be given, the officers started bludgeoning groups of boys and girls with clubs and cattle prodders, which give a severe shock and leave burn marks on the flesh."

After this and other horrifying incidents in Americus—including the police shooting of James Brown, a Black veteran who had dared to walk through a white neighborhood—SNCC activists wrote down eyewitness accounts and delivered them to the FBI, the investigative arm of the Department of Justice.

"It must have been the cops that the FBI chose to believe," a SNCC leader said later. "For, despite a mountain of evidence like those affidavits, the Justice Department managed to announce on August 12 that it had uncovered 'no evidence of police brutality.'"

One Reason Why They March!

Here is one of the several reasons civil rights advocates took their cause into the streets in a mammoth March on Washington seeking support of the President's Civil Rights package this week.

In the photo an unidentified man grimaces in pain as a Louisiana State Trooper touches him on the back with an electric cattle prod to hurry his departure from a demonstration around the City Hall in Plaquemine, La., on Aug. 22.

Being sought in the Civil Rights package before Congress is freedom from police brutality. Over 284 were arrested—by means pictured here—in the Louisiana hamlet.

Shocks from the cattle prods left burn marks on the skin of protesters.

The August 12 announcement fueled the picketing now outside the DOJ building. But the protesters were also furious about the department's recent decision to charge nine Black activists in Albany, Georgia, with the crime of intimidating a federal juror.

Two facts in the case were clear: (1) the protesters had picketed a grocery store owned by a white man; and (2) the owner had served on a jury that found a white sheriff not guilty of the charge of murdering a

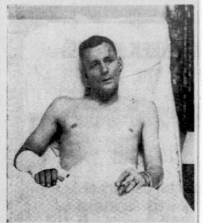

SENECA—Imperial Grand Wizard and Grand Dragon Robert M. Shelton of the Alabama Ku Klux Klan, who got a broken arm and other minor injuries in a plane crash near here Monday, is shown in Oconee Memorial Hospital here. Shelton and a companion, Frederick G. Smith, left the hospital Tuesday morning.

Won't Continue To Washington

Klansman To Go To Pilot's Rites

By DOUGLAS MAULDIN
News Staff Writer

WALHALLA — A top-ranking Alabama Ku Klux Klan leader, injured in a plane crash near here Monday, was discharged from a hospital Tuesday morning and announced he would not continue to his original destination, Washington, D. C., where a civil rights march is scheduled Wednesday.

Instead, Robert M. Shelton, imperial grand wizard and grand dragon of the Alabama Ku Klux Klan, said he would go to Madisonville, Ky., for funeral services of Alvin D. Sisk, pilot of the ill-fated craft.

Sisk, 350-p o u n d man who escaped barely alive early Monday afternoon with Shelton and Frederick G. Smith, all of Tuscaloosa, Ala., died in Oconee Memorial Hospital in Seneca at 3:15 a.m. Tuesday.

Shelton and Smith, who had lesser injuries, pulled the pilot from the wreckage.

Oconee County Coroner Floyd Owens said Sisk's death was caused by head and chest injuries.

The single engined plane, probing for a break in dense fog cloaking the mountainous area at the time, smashed into trees on Medlin Mountain 25 miles north of Walhalla.

Coroner Owens empaneled a jury but said he did not know whether an inquest would be necessary.

Davenport Funeral Home of Walhalla shipped Sisk's body to his mother's home in Madisonville, according to hospital authorities.

EN ROUTE TO SPARTANBURG

When the Cessna Skylane cracked up about 1:30 p.m. 75 yards off U. S. Highway 107, the three men were en route to Spartanburg, where they said they were to

pick up a fourth passenger, identified as Bob Scoggins, active with Piedmont area Klan affairs.

Accompanied by Scoggins, Shelton and Smith appeared at Sheriff D. H. (Buck) Crenshaw's office early Tuesday afternoon. They talked with the sheriff and the coroner and indicated they would be glad to assist in any way possible with investigation of the crash.

They said their immediate concern was with the family of the dead pilot and they planned to attend his funeral services.

Coroner Owens said Shelton and Smith blamed a faulty altimeter with the accident. They said Sisk had dropped the light craft down from 11,000 feet to 4,500 feet searching for an opening in the fog when they suddenly hit the trees, 40 minutes out of Chattanooga, Tenn., their last refueling stop.

The pilot was apparently unaware of the highway's presence, as visibility at ground level Monday afternoon w a s extremely limited. The plane skimmed over the road by about 100 feet before slicing a path 15 yards wide into the trees.

Investigators of the Federal Aviation Agency and the S. C. Aeronautics Commission came to the scene Tuesday to determine officially why the plane fell.

The roped-off wreckage in a clump of trees was under guard by Civil Defense auxiliary police and Sheriff Crenshaw's deputies all night.

"BUSINESS TRIP"

Shelton nor Scoggins would reveal the purpose of the Washington trip, except to say it was a "business trip."

Scoggins, a Spartanburg plumber, indicated he would continue on to the Capital City, however. Sheriff Crenshaw said about 75 Ku Klux Klan pamphlets were in the plane's wreckage.

Black man. Less clear was the answer to the question of whether the two facts were related. Did the protesters picket the store *because* the owner had voted to acquit the sheriff?

The demonstrators claimed that their protest was about racial inequality at the store, not about the owner's jury service, but DOJ investigators didn't believe them, so they pursued federal indictments of the nine Black activists. It was the first time in the 1960s that the DOJ targeted Black civil rights activists for federal prosecution—and SNCC was incensed.

At the picketing outside the DOJ, SNCC organizer Bob Moses carried a sign that read, "When There Is No Justice, What Is the State but a Robber Band Enlarged?"

Moses stayed put, but a handful of picketers peeled away and marched to the White House. They wanted President Kennedy to know that they found him just as guilty as his brother in failing to advance justice for Black people.

Malcolm X said that Allah struck down the plane carrying the KKK leader.

While SNCC picketed and Kennedy dined, freedom trains from Chicago and other cities continued to roll toward Washington. One of the trains had started in Jacksonville, Florida, and was now making stops in Georgia, South Carolina, North Carolina, and Virginia.

Patricia Due, the CORE leader in Tallahassee, Florida, rode the rails with her husband, John, a law school student, and young activists from CORE and SNCC. Many of them had been arrested and brutalized by white police officers, and police brutality was their main concern as they chatted about the march.

According to John, SNCC and CORE activists "were going to the march to demand that Kennedy and the federal government pass a civil rights bill and use its national police powers to protect black people."

The activists were "angry in mood," John said, but they also felt a "joyous excitement" as they belted out freedom songs on their way to Washington.

Also on this busy eve of the march, Malcolm X held an informal press conference at the Statler Hotel, where the Big Ten, along with other march organizers, met behind closed doors.

Two days earlier, Malcolm had appeared on CBS-TV and repeated his claim that the march had "been

After March Day, Malcolm referred to the protest as the "Farce on Washington."

taken over by the government . . . is being controlled by the government and is being used for political expediency."

The Nation of Islam minister also ridiculed the march's plan to rally at the Lincoln Memorial. President Lincoln was no hero, Malcolm said. "Had he freed the slaves, we wouldn't have any race problem."

Now, standing in the lobby of the Statler Hotel, Malcolm criticized the march leaders for "seeking favors from 'the white man's government.'" He also called the march a "fiasco" and predicted that "an explosion" would occur if spectators lost patience with being "pushed around" by the marchers.

Rather than marching to a "dead man's statue," Malcolm advised, Black people should join the Nation of Islam and demand the creation of an "all-black" state.

It was a tough sell, and about two hundred thousand Black folks would soon ignore his advice.

Some had already arrived, and as a half-moon rose in the night sky, they climbed the marble steps of the Lincoln Memorial and read the words of the Emancipation Proclamation. Tomorrow, they would use their own voices to demand—and proclaim—freedom for all.

WE DEMAND AN END TO POLICE BRUTALITY?

Near the end of July, Martin Luther King, Jr., had told the media that march organizers intended to ask President Kennedy to create "a federal civil rights police force" to protect demonstrators in the country from police brutality. In addition, the demands in the first version of the organizing manual (see page 105) listed "an end to police brutality directed against citizens using their constitutional right of peaceful demonstration." Below is the list of demands published in the final organizing booklet. To this day, it's not clear what happened to the demand about police brutality. Why do you think it was deleted? Compare these ten demands to the earlier ones. Is this list stronger or weaker than the first? Or is it about the same?

WHAT WE DEMAND*

1. Comprehensive and effective *civil rights legislation* from the present Congress—without compromise or filibuster—to guarantee all Americans
        access to all public accommodations
        decent housing
        adequate and integrated education
        the right to vote

2. Withholding of Federal funds from all programs in which discrimination exists.

3. *Desegregation of all school districts in 1963.*

4. Enforcement of the *Fourteenth Amendment*—reducing Congressional representation of states where citizens are disfranchised.

5. A new *Executive Order* banning discrimination in all housing supported by federal funds.

6. Authority for the Attorney General to institute *injunctive suits* when any constiutional right is violated.

7. A massive federal program to train and place all unemployed workers—Negro and white—on meaningful and dignified jobs at decent wages.

8. A national *minimum wage* act that will give all Americans a decent standard of living. (Government surveys show that anything less than $2.00 an hour fails to do this.)

9. A broadened *Fair Labor Standards Act* to include all areas of employment which are presently excluded.

10. A federal *Fair Employment Practices Act* barring discrimination by federal, state, and municipal governments, and by employers, contractors, employment agencies, and trade unions.

*Support of the March does not necessarily indicate endorsement of every demand listed. Some organizations have not had an opportunity to take an official position on all of the demands advocated here.

4

In 1963, twenty-three-year-old John Lewis became chairman of the Student Nonviolent Coordinating Committee (SNCC).

14

MILITANT VOICES

John Lewis returned to his hotel room late at night. Opening the door, he saw a handwritten note lying on the floor.

"John, come downstairs," it read. "Must see you at once."

The note was from Bayard Rustin.

Lewis sensed something was wrong, and his fears were confirmed when Rustin called a few seconds later.

"It's your speech," Rustin explained. "Some people are very concerned about some of the things you're going to say in your speech. You need to get down here. We need to talk."

Earlier in the evening, SNCC staffer Courtland Cox had placed copies of Lewis's speech on a press table. Cox had helped craft the speech, he was proud of it, and he wanted to share it with the media.

Somehow, a copy ended up in the hands of Archbishop Patrick O'Boyle, the white Catholic leader of Washington, DC, who was scheduled to deliver the invocation, or opening prayer, at the march. O'Boyle wasn't happy with what he read, and he called Rustin with a threat.

If Lewis doesn't change his speech, I won't offer the invocation.

Even before Rustin's call, Lewis understood that moderates, especially friends and confidants of President Kennedy, like O'Boyle and Walter Reuther, would find plenty of material in his speech to disparage.

After all, Lewis planned to say: "In good conscience, we cannot support wholeheartedly the administration's civil rights bill, for it is too little and too late. There is not one thing in the bill that will protect our people from police brutality."

Lewis also knew that his use of the word "revolution" might set off alarms among those who opposed disruptive tactics and civil disobedience.

Then, there was this fiery section: "We will march through the South, through the heart of Dixie, the way Sherman did. We shall pursue our own 'scorched earth' policy and burn Jim Crow to the ground—nonviolently." Lewis was referring here to Union General William Tecumseh Sherman and the scorched-earth campaign he had waged during the Civil War.

Downstairs, Rustin told Lewis that the most urgent problem was the way he described "patience."

Seeing Lewis's surprise, Rustin pointed to the part under question: "To those who have said, 'Be patient and wait,' we must say that 'patience' is a dirty and nasty word. We cannot be patient, we do not want to be free gradually. We want our freedom, and we want it *now*."

"This is offensive to the Catholic Church," Rustin said. "Catholics *believe* in the word 'patience.'"

Lewis understood that Catholics had long extolled patience as a virtue for believers hoping for the end of times. So, although hesitant, he agreed to delete his description of patience as "a dirty and nasty word."

Rustin was pleased, but he also warned Lewis that he might have to deal with more objections the following morning.

"By the time I got back to my room, I was incensed," Lewis recalled.

He liked his speech just as it was—radical, militant, impatient—and as he climbed into bed and closed his eyes, he resolved to protect every word of it.

At 3:40 a.m., while Lewis slept, CORE-sponsored buses in Harlem

*On August 28, New York City bus passengers
left for the march well before dawn.*

took off for Washington. Sue Brookway of Chappaqua, New York, felt
a bolt of excitement as she stood in the dimly lit aisle of Bus 10.

"I think the biggest influence of the march will be to create a greater
national awareness of the issue and get more people to make a commitment to the cause," she told bus captain George Johnson.

Nearby, passenger Omar Ahmed grew annoyed. The march, he believed, wasn't about raising awareness, especially among white liberals
like Brookway. The march was about *forcing* the government to ensure
jobs and freedom for Black folks *now*.

Captain Johnson seemed less annoyed than resigned, especially
about the civil rights bill now stalled in Congress. "I don't think the civil
rights bill will get through," he said. "I have no faith in the white man."

The bus captain apparently put his faith in a more militant approach,
even in those who, like Malcolm X, denounced nonviolent tactics. "[A]s

far as I'm concerned, anything done to get our rights is OK," Johnson declared.

Omar Ahmed agreed, and he jumped into the conversation, directing his comments at Brockway and other white passengers within earshot. "The white power structure has bred a New Negro, and he is angry and impatient," said Ahmed. "It's not just the Black Muslims [Nation of Islam members]. It's the man on the street. Come down to Harlem some night and listen to what's being said on the street corners. The cops go through, and you can see fear on their faces. This isn't Birmingham. If anyone starts anything, we won't be passive."

Brookway and other white passengers didn't know how to reply, and that wasn't the end of it.

As the bus weaved through heavy predawn traffic, the conversation focused again on white liberals and their contributions to the Black freedom movement.

When white passenger Frank Harman offered that he wanted to join the Peace Corps and help Black people in Nigeria, Wayne Kinsler, a nineteen-year-old Black man, felt his face growing hot.

"I want to go help these people because they are human beings," Harman explained.

Kinsler erupted.

"If this thing [the civil rights movement] comes to violence, yours will be the first throat we slit," he growled at Harman. "We don't need your kind . . . We don't need any white liberals to patronize us!"

"We don't trust you!" another voice yelled above the din of the bus engine.

Harman was shocked and confused. *What did I say that set these guys off?*

"We've been stabbed in the back too many times," explained another rider. Perhaps he was talking about white liberal politicians who promised jobs and freedom but then caved in the face of white supremacy. Or about unfulfilled commitments from other white people, everyone from schoolteachers to factory owners.

Stunned, Harman sat in silence.

CORE member James Peck was badly beaten during the historic 1961 Freedom Rides.

Also aboard Bus 10 was James Peck.

Like the young Black passengers, he knew all about white leaders who said one thing and did another. And he, too, felt the pain of betrayal.

But Peck was white—and a veteran CORE member with a remarkable history. In 1961, he'd volunteered for the Freedom Rides, and with John Lewis by his side, he'd been beaten by white supremacists wielding pipes, chains, and baseball bats. A huge gash on his head required fifty-three stitches.

Peck's presence on Bus 10 bore silent witness to one of CORE's fundamental beliefs—that some white people were trustworthy and would fight hard, even to death, for civil rights.

Perhaps CORE leader James Farmer would have pointed to Peck during the intense discussion now taking place. But Farmer was behind bars in Plaquemine, Louisiana, for leading an interracial protest of racial segregation.

CORE founder James Farmer expressed regret for not speaking at the march, though he also believed that remaining in jail was the right thing to do.

A member of the Big Six, Farmer was scheduled to be a main speaker at the Lincoln Memorial rally. But he wasn't going anywhere. Sure, he could make bail and head to the nation's capital in time for the rally, but there was no way he would leave his colleagues behind.

Without Farmer's voice to guide them, the Black and white riders on Bus 10 talked past one another until they ran out of steam. Eventually, snoring, whispers, and the soft chewing of cookies and fruit replaced all the shouting.

Those still awake peered out their windows and saw a massive cara-
van of vehicles—buses, cars, and trucks—heading to the march. Many
of the buses were decorated with colorful "Freedom-Now!" banners.

People of all colors smiled and waved.

PART FOUR
GATHERING
AND MARCHING

*New York City CORE activists arriving at
Union Station in Washington*

4 Thurmond Assistants Pack Pistols

Banner Washington Bureau

Washington—Four men on Sen. Strom Thurmond's staff are "packing" pistols to work because of threats against the life of the South Carolina Democrat who is an outspoken foe of President Kennedy's civil rights bill.

One assistant said several telephone calls have warned that Thurmond might be a target for attack during the "March on Washington."

"We are packing pistols but the senator himself has no gun and he's not asking for any special police protection," one assistant said. "He says he won't be intimidated by any threats or reports of threats. Our office is open today. But we are letting the girls on the staff stay home."

The first threats were telephone calls to the senator's apartment at night, during the Senate Commerce hearings on the civil rights bill. These were dismissed as the work of "cranks."

In the past few days, however, friends in Philadelphia and New York relayed serious warnings that an attempt would be made to "get Thurmond" today.

Thurmond, a major general in the Army Reserve and a combat veteran of the Normandy landings, will carry on his Senate work as usual, his assistants said.

Senator Thurmond's staffers resolved to protect their boss from reported death threats.

15

RISING AT DAWN

Before sunrise on Wednesday, August 28, Martin Niverth polished his black shoes and checked his revolver. By 6:00 a.m., he was at the Metropolitan Police Department's downtown garage, where his commander told him that he was responsible for policing an area along the National Mall. Everything seemed like a typical workday—until Niverth learned who his partner would be.

His name was William Wallace. He was a rookie. And he was Black.

Niverth was stunned. He was used to having a white partner. Although the Washington Police Department had white and Black officers, they rarely patrolled together.

Surprised by their assignment, Niverth and Wallace greeted each other and began walking toward the National Mall.

For these two officers, it was already a historic day.

As the glowing sun peeked over the horizon, Bayard Rustin strolled around the grounds of the Washington Monument. He wanted to see the results of eight weeks of planning.

Things looked fantastic! About two hundred portable toilets, twenty-one portable water fountains, eight 2,500-gallon water tanks, and thirty-five first-aid stations dotted the area around the Washington Monument and the Lincoln Memorial.

And, perhaps best of all, the sound system was working! Rustin had asked for the best system available, one that would allow speakers at the

Lincoln Memorial to be heard by everyone between the Memorial and the Washington Monument.

"We cannot maintain order where people cannot hear," he'd explained.

His plan for a first-rate sound system had almost gone up in smoke. During the night, someone had sabotaged the system. It took engineers from the Army Signal Corps, compliments of the federal government, to save the day.

Although everything seemed in good order, one vital ingredient was missing.

Where are all the people? Rustin wondered.

Only a few hundred were milling about, hardly a good sign, and Rustin panicked a bit, imagining that staff projections were wrong. Yes,

Anticipating huge crowds, the Kennedy administration sought to keep the march orderly by arranging for the presence of a massive police force, including military police.

they *thought* more than one hundred thousand marchers would show up, but did they know *for sure*?

Members of the press spotted Rustin as he surveyed the grounds, and they approached him with the same question. *Where are all the people?*

Rustin pulled a piece of paper out of his suit jacket, looked at it closely, and checked his pocket watch. Then, using his most sophisticated accent, he declared: "Gentleman, everything is going exactly according to plan."

But the paper wasn't a schedule at all—it was blank! Rustin had faked it, and successfully. Although the media were now assured that a massive crowd would show up, the deputy director continued to imagine a march without marchers.

As the sun rose a bit more, Aquilla Bateman ignored the instruction for marchers to gather at the Washington Monument. She was seventy-four years old, she suffered from a bad leg, and she wanted the best view possible at the Lincoln Memorial.

Bateman was probably the first marcher at the Memorial. She was also deeply religious, and she bowed her head in prayer.

"O Lord, be with us today and keep us in the hollow of your hand. May we get together. I pray that nobody will do anything personal bad to anybody else in Washington today."

While Bateman prayed for peace, the city started to resemble a police state, a country controlled by the military. About 1,900 DC police officers were now on active duty. Joining them were 2,500 National Guard officers, 430 firefighters, 500 police reservists, and 300 National Park officers. It was the largest security operation in the history of the nation's capital.

Also, Army jeeps rumbled through the streets, and an Army helicopter hovered just above the tree line. About 4,000 troops at Fort

Myer, two miles outside the District, stood ready for quick deployment, and 15,000 paratroopers of the 82nd Airborne Division, based in Fort Bragg, North Carolina, were prepared to fly into action.

Atop the Lincoln Memorial, Justice Department officials positioned cameras so they could surveil the crowd, and Army officers crouched into secret positions.

Despite all the warnings that the march was a ticking time bomb, Aquilla Bateman had come. Finding her choice spot, she sat down, trusting that this special day, with God's help, would be peaceful and inspiring.

Volunteer marshals, trained in nonviolence, using a walkie-talkie to monitor crowd safety

WHY SO MANY SECURITY OFFICERS?

Washington was used to large crowds. The 1952 and 1956 presidential inaugurations each drew 750,000 visitors, and the annual July Fourth fireworks display usually attracted 250,000. And yet there had never been a larger security operation than the one planned for the upcoming march. Some folks cried foul, suggesting that the massive operation was the result of a racist belief that large crowds of Black people would inevitably become unruly. But DC Police Chief Robert V. Murray said there was a "crucial difference" between the march crowd and earlier ones. "Those were crowds of spectators," he said. "We do not expect any spectators during the march. They will all be participants, on one side or the other, or they would not be there." Do you find his statement convincing? Or do you believe the massive security operation was a manifestation of racism?

George Rockwell, the American Nazi leader, had already picked his spot, too. He and about forty followers, many of them teenagers, were stationed on the outer edges of the Washington Monument grounds.

"We are here on behalf of the white Christian majority," Rockwell told reporters.

A day earlier, the group had staged a protest in nearby Rockville, Maryland, wearing their full stormtrooper regalia—brown uniforms and hats, black belts and boots, and swastikas—but this morning they were in regular clothes.

Rockwell had applied for a permit to hold a counterdemonstration at the march, but the city promptly denied it, leaving the American Nazis to be nothing more than spectators.

Nevertheless, the Nazi leader claimed that he oversaw about a hundred security troops who would infiltrate the march and be on the lookout for trouble.

"My men will aid the police in suppressing the black mob," Rockwell said.

But that plan quickly collapsed. Fifty police officers, Black and white, soon formed a circle around Rockwell and his men. The Nazis weren't going anywhere.

But thousands upon thousands of marchers were well on their way—on 2,173 buses, 21 chartered trains, 6 chartered planes, and an unknown number of cars, motorcycles, and bikes.

On a plane from Los Angeles, "the mood was one of determination," according to a *New York Times* reporter.

ROLLER MAN

Ledger Smith wanted to dramatize the importance of the march by using his best skill—roller-skating. On Saturday, August 17, the twenty-seven-year-old truck driver went to the NAACP office in Chicago, put on his black roller skates, and took off for Washington. NAACP members escorted him by car on the 700-mile trip. Known as "Roller Man," Smith wore a "Freedom" banner and attracted a lot of attention along the way. Most of it was friendly and supportive. But one mean-spirited man tried to make him crash. When Roller Man arrived in Washington on Tuesday, August 27, he was shaky, sore, and ten pounds lighter.

Ledger Smith replaced his wheels several times on the trip to Washington.

"You can never know what it's like to be a Negro," a Black woman told her seatmate. "No matter how hard you try, you can't imagine going into a hamburger shop with your children and being told, 'We don't serve niggers here.'"

On a train from New York, joyful passengers sang one freedom song after another—"We Shall Overcome," "We Won't Be Left Behind," and "Freedom, Freedom!"

And on a bus from Alabama, Black passengers beamed when a Black officer in Washington—a *Black* officer!—gave them parking directions.

"Now that's what I call good police work!" remarked a happy rider.

As they all drew closer to the center of action, transportation captains reminded their groups of the seriousness of the cause that lay ahead. Some of the bus captains stood in the center aisles and read "An Appeal By the March Leaders":

The Washington March of Aug. 28 is more than just a demonstration. It was conceived as an outpouring of deep feeling of millions of white and colored American citizens that the time has come for the Government of the United States of America . . . to grant and guarantee complete equality in citizenship to the Negro minority of our populations . . .

It will be orderly, but not subservient. It will be proud, but not arrogant. It will be nonviolent, but not timid. It will be unified in purposes and behavior, not splintered . . . It will be outspoken, but not raucous . . .

We, the undersigned [Big Ten], who see the Washington March as wrapping up the dreams, hopes, ambitions, tears and prayers of millions who have lived for this day, call upon the members, followers and well-wishers of our several organizations to make the March a disciplined and purposeful demonstration . . . We call for self-discipline, so that no one in our own ranks, however enthusiastic, shall be the spark for disorder . . .

We ask each and every one in attendance in Washington, or in spiritual attendance back home, to place the cause above all else . . .

Let's win at Washington.

JAMES BALDWIN AND THE WALK IN PARIS

On August 21, novelist James Baldwin and a group of eighty white and Black Americans staged a walk from the American Church in Paris to the nearby US embassy. Baldwin called it a "walk" rather than a "march" because of a ban on public demonstrations. The purpose of the walk was to demonstrate solidarity with the upcoming March on Washington. "We want to serve notice we are part of this revolution in the United States," Baldwin said. At the embassy, the group presented a US official with a fifteen-foot-long scroll signed by hundreds of Americans living abroad. The scroll denounced segregation, endorsed the march, and called for passage of the civil rights bill.

16

THE OCCUPATION BEGINS

Actors Ossie Davis and Ruby Dee had the usual jitters. The married couple were scheduled to be emcees for two entertainment programs at the march, one at the Washington Monument and a later one at the Lincoln Memorial. As they dressed for the big day, they heard a rap on their hotel door.

Who could that be? they wondered.

Opening the door, Davis saw their good friend—Malcolm X.

Davis and Dee weren't completely surprised. They had spotted Malcolm yesterday, while he was speaking with a reporter who asked why he had showed up for the march.

"Well," Malcolm said, "whatever Black folks do, maybe I don't agree with any of it, [but] I'm going to be there, brother, 'cause that's where I belong."

Davis and Dee welcomed their friend with big smiles and asked the reason for his surprise visit.

I want you to know that if you need help on anything, I am here to help, Malcolm said.

The Nation of Islam minister had already assured march leaders that he and his followers would

Ruby Dee and Ossie Davis, emcees for the entertainment programs, were friends with Malcolm X.

The Washington
Monument casting
its morning shadow
over early arrivals

do nothing to provoke violence, and now he was taking an extra step with Davis. *If there's violence and I can help, tell me. I'll do anything.*

Davis and Dee thanked him for the kind offer, and Malcolm was soon out the door. He didn't want to miss a thing.

A gigantic green tent near the Washington Monument served as march headquarters, and as of 7:00 a.m., it was open for business.

March volunteers raised money by selling souvenir booklets.

Inside, march marshals pulled on yellow armbands marked with the letter "M," checked last-minute instructions for keeping order, and tested their walkie-talkies. Code names like "Freedom" and "Justice" were assigned.

Other adult volunteers divided into groups of fifteen and put on purple armbands that read "USHER." Their job was to sell buttons, pennants, and programs, and distribute cards for marchers to sign and return. The cards invited the marchers to pledge themselves to use non-violence in the fight for social justice.

Nearby, transportation director Rachelle Horowitz took calls from travelers who were stranded with broken-down vehicles, or who had some other vexing problem. Her reply was always the same—*See if you can hitch a ride!*

And outside the tent, Bob Avery and his friends stood near the thousands of signs they had put together during the past week. Their hands were sore from all the stapling, but they couldn't have been prouder to see the signs ready to go. No other march on Washington had ever used so many signs to share protest messages.

Handing out some of the tens of thousands of signs that communicated the march's political demands

Up at the Lincoln Memorial, Aquilla Bateman looked behind her.

Several thousand people were now at the Washington Monument, lounging on the grass, eating sandwiches, taking naps. Thousands more would soon arrive. Around 8:00 a.m., buses were passing through the Baltimore Harbor Tunnel at the rate of one hundred per hour, and chartered trains were beginning to pull into Union Station.

Jean Shepherd, a popular radio host, was on a bus from Philadelphia. On the outskirts of Washington, in some of the poorer areas, he saw lots of residents on their porches—"little old ladies, grandmas, skinny kids, tough-looking men who worked as garage mechanics, nuns." Smiling and waving, they were the city's unofficial welcoming committee.

There was a different feel downtown. There, the city seemed eerily quiet, as if it was a Sunday rather than a Wednesday.

New York Times reporter Russell Baker observed that "the downtown streets were empty." Half of all retail shops were closed. Bars and liquor stores—banned from selling alcohol for the day—also had locked doors. And countless government workers had chosen to stay home. Perhaps they feared violence or wanted to avoid traffic jams. Or maybe they opposed the march and didn't want to be anywhere near it.

"For the natives, this was obviously a day of siege and the streets were being left to the marchers," Baker wrote.

At 9:30 a.m., 40,000 marchers were at the Washington Monument.

Eighteen-year-old Eric Kulberg, an intern at the Department of the Interior, asked his boss, who was also white, for the day off.

"What are you, a nigger lover or something?" the boss wondered.

"I guess so," Kulberg replied.

Granted permission, the young man eagerly headed to the roof so he could snap photographs of the arriving marchers.

At Union Station, eighteen-year-old Francine Yeager stepped off the Freedom Train from Chicago. Like countless others, she'd been inspired to attend the march after seeing the Birmingham students brutalized by Bull Connor and his police dogs.

Yeager was too impatient to wait for a shuttle, so she grabbed her best friend, Florestine, and joined the hordes hoofing their way to the Monument.

*Crowds of marchers at Union
Station in Washington*

The sights and sounds were overwhelming.

My goodness—a Black woman and a white man holding hands! And over there! That older white man just said "excuse me" to a Black teenager!

"Florestine," Francine declared, "this is what heaven's gonna be like when we get there."

On a street near the Monument, Black reporter Malverse Nicholson watched long lines at food trucks and concession stands selling hot dogs, soda, and chips. The most popular vendor, even at this early hour, was the man scooping Good Humor ice cream.

Nicholson also focused his sights on the Black vendor whose table was full of books, magazines, and postcards featuring Black people. By far, the bestselling book was James Baldwin's *Another Country*, a controversial novel that described interracial love, Black rage, and gay sexuality.

It was selling like hotcakes.

At the Washington Monument, reporters thought that the grounds resembled a church picnic—lots of lounging and laughing and smiling and backslapping. Jean Shepherd said it felt like a "family reunion."

But a closer look showed that there was a lot more than the "holiday mood" that Shepherd saw. There was also a militant mood.

The SNCC activists who had picketed the Department of Justice now held their protest signs on Monument grounds. One sign read, "Milton Wilkerson—20 stitches. Emanuel McClendon—3 stitches (Age 67). James Williams—broken leg." They were the names and injuries of people beaten by the police during civil rights demonstrations in Americus, Georgia.

Nearby, eighteen-year-old James Lee Pruitt, a Black SNCC worker from Mississippi, carried a sign that read, "Stop Criminal Prosecutions of Voter Registration Workers in Mississippi."

Pruitt knew all about his sign. He and other SNCC workers had

Preparing for the day outside march headquarters

recently been jailed for trying to organize and register Black voters. In their jail cells, they were forced to sit nude with a fan pointed directly at them. When one SNCC worker grew ill and asked for a doctor, a jail guard said, "Sure, nigger, after you are dead."

On the sloping hill next to the Monument, about seventy-five young activists from Danville, Virginia, shared other bone-chilling stories of brutality. A few months earlier, when they were protesting for civil rights, police officers had clubbed them, and firefighters had trained hoses on them, until they couldn't stand up. It felt like Birmingham all over again. Now, they wore black mourning armbands and mournfully sang, "Move on, move on, move on with the freedom fight."

And in front of the headquarters tent, a group of Black teenagers summoned the memory of Medgar Evers and Jackson, Mississippi. Wearing CORE T-shirts, the teens formed a circle and sang a freedom

CORE marchers were upset about police brutality in
Louisiana, where some of their members remained in jail.

song called "I'm Gonna Sit at the Welcome Table," but they changed the lyrics to express their resolve to transform the violent city.

"I'm going to walk the streets of Jackson," one girl sang.

"One of these days," her friend sang in reply.

"I'm going to be the Chief of Police," another girl sang.

"One of these days," the CORE teens replied.

Like James Pruitt and the Danville teens, the CORE kids weren't on a holiday break. They were in Washington to tell the world about white violence against Black people. So while the gathering at the Monument felt like a picnic to some, to these radical young activists it was a time to express anger and frustration, pain and suffering, resolve and determination.

It was a time to be themselves—militant and on the march.

The demand for voting rights appeared on official and unofficial signs.

17

BLACK WOMEN SPEAK, HATEMONGERS RAGE

An attentive marshal looked at James Pruitt's homemade sign—the one calling for the government to stop prosecuting voter registration workers in Mississippi.

"Has that sign been approved?" asked the marshal.

"It's my sign," Pruitt replied.

That was an unsatisfying answer, and the marshal asked Pruitt to accompany him to march headquarters. The marshal wasn't mean like the police officers in Mississippi. He was simply, and politely, trying to enforce a regulation stated in *Organizing Manual No. 2:* "All slogans carried in this March will be designed exclusively by the National Committee and will be distributed at the Washington Monument."

Bayard Rustin insisted on this rule so he could control the march's message and keep out slogans from groups who were at odds with the march, like communists and Nazis.

Inside headquarters, the chief marshal read Pruitt's sign and asked for an explanation.

The SNCC worker recounted the horrifying time he had spent in jail for registering voters. He also offered that he had abandoned his car on the way to the march because no one in the white area where it had broken down would service it.

The chief quickly concluded that Pruitt was neither a communist

Hundreds of Black students from Virginia's Prince Edward County marched for the desegregation of their public schools.

nor a Nazi. He was, by all counts, one of those militant SNCC workers who sacrificed their livelihoods—and their lives—for the sake of Black freedom.

You're free to carry your sign, the chief said.

Walking out of the green tent, Pruitt saw a long line of people waiting to snag one of the official march signs.

Nearby, more than a hundred Black students from Prince Edward County in Virginia lit up when they saw signs demanding the *immediate* integration of schools. Five years earlier, their all-white school board had decided to close all public schools rather than integrate them, as required by law. Although hundreds of Black children left the county to study in other places, poor kids didn't have the resources to leave, and they suffered without any public education.

But right now, the students stood in awe of the Washington Monument, the White House, and all the people who believed what they did—that children had the right to attend integrated public schools. Their chaperone told a reporter that the kids were "overjoyed" to be at the march. The students also demonstrated fierce resolve as they sang,

We are soldiers in the army.
We have to fight, although we have to cry.
We have to hold up the blood-stained banner.
We have to hold it up until we die!

"Oh, freedom."

The beautiful voice with the clearest of tones came from the entertainment stage, a couple hundred yards away from the Monument. The growing crowd there grew relatively quiet as folk singer Joan Baez continued with her song:

Oh, freedom.
Oh, freedom over me.
Before I'll be a slave,
I'll be buried in my grave
And go home to my Lord and be free.

Folk singer Joan Baez, part of the entertainment
program at the Washington Monument

It was 10:00 a.m., the sun was up, and about ninety thousand people now overflowed the Washington Monument grounds, crossed over Constitution Avenue, and spilled onto the Ellipse, a grassy oval area behind the White House. Thousands more were still on the way.

Walking from Georgetown, Diana Zentay and her roommate, both recent college graduates, felt unsure—and fearful. Today's march would mark the first time that Zentay protested for civil rights, and she was concerned about the possibility of violence.

"We did not know whether we were going to make it back alive," Zentay recalled. "There was fear. Who knows what would happen, but I said, 'Do we believe this or not?'"

The two white women believed, and they walked on.

WHERE ARE THE JAZZ MUSICIANS?

Why do you think jazz was not included in the musical offerings at the Washington Monument and the Lincoln Memorial? Black Americans had played a prominent role in the historic development of jazz, and in 1963 some of the most popular musicians in the United States were Black jazz artists—for example, Duke Ellington, Nina Simone, Dizzy Gillespie, and Sarah Vaughan.

"I'm on my way," sang Odetta, who'd followed Baez on the entertainment stage. The marchers seemed captivated by her remarkably deep voice and the passion it expressed.

Close to center stage was Josh White, a singer known for his militant songs about racial injustice and white violence against Black people. In 1940, Joshua White and His Carolinians—a newly formed group— had released an album titled *Chain Gang*. The first stanza of the first

song set the album's radical tone: "Well, I always been in trouble, 'cause I'm a black-skinned man."

Singing first tenor on that hard-hitting album was none other than Bayard Rustin. Now, twenty-three years later, Rustin was offering White the biggest stage of his career. The talented singer couldn't wait. Grabbing his guitar, he jumped onstage and joined Odetta in mid song. After she sang a line, he repeated it in a bluesy, gravelly voice.

> *I'm on my way*
> *I'm on my way.*
> *And I won't turn back.*
> *And I won't turn back.*

Soon, all the other scheduled singers joined Odetta and White onstage, and as they finished the freedom song, the crowd roared.

No one was turning back!

An older woman in the crowd smiled. She loved all of Odetta's songs—they were her favorites—and Odetta loved her back, partly because of everything she had done for the movement.

On the evening of December 1, 1955, this woman was on a bus in Montgomery, Alabama.

"Let me have those front seats," barked the white bus driver.

The four Black passengers didn't budge. They knew it was legal for drivers to make them surrender their seats in the "whites only" section, but they still resented the injustice.

Driver James Blake was now agitated. He wanted the four riders—three women and a man—to vacate their seats for the one white man standing in the aisle.

"You all better make it light on yourselves and let me have those seats," Blake said.

Three stood up, but one refused. The stubborn one, Rosa Parks, was a soft-spoken seamstress at the Montgomery Fair Department Store. She was also a veteran leader in the Montgomery branch of the NAACP.

Parks slid from her aisle seat to the window seat,

Rosa Parks speaking at the Washington Monument gathering

giving the white passenger three easy choices. But even that did not satisfy Blake, and he marched back to Parks.

"Are you going to stand up?" he asked.

Parks looked him in the eye.

"No," she said.

Now, eight years later, Rosa Parks was standing up for freedom again.

Around 11:00 a.m., with the crowd still swelling, Bayard Rustin appeared front and center on the entertainment stage.

"Ladies and gentlemen," he announced, "I want to introduce to you the woman who started our modern struggle for freedom because she got tired of indignity and Jim Crow and sat down. And when Rosa Parks sat down, a revolution broke forth!"

Parks smiled and offered just a few words.

"Hello, friends of freedom," she said. "It's a wonderful day and let us be thankful we have reached this point, and we go forward now to greater things. Thank you."

March organizer Anna Arnold Hedgeman appreciated the moment, but she still thought that her fellow march planners had failed to give Parks her due. If Hedgeman had her way, Wednesday, August 28, would be called "Rosa Parks Day."

Rustin then introduced the leader of the Little Rock, Arkansas, battle for school desegregation—Daisy Bates. Speaking without notes, Bates thanked the crowd from the bottom of her heart.

This is indeed a happy day for me. You know, sometimes in your life when you are fighting for freedom and human dignity your faith fails you, and you wonder whether democracy is worth fighting for, or whether you can ever be an American citizen in this country. But something happens that renews faith in democracy and in America and its people. It happened to me in 1957 when the students of Little Rock walked alone through the mob. You cried with us, but we had to walk it alone. But your presence here today testifies that no child will have to walk alone through a mob in any city or hamlet of this country because you will be there walking with them. Thank you.

On the fringes of the massive crowd, American Nazi leader George Lincoln Rockwell ranted and raged about Black people. But Rockwell was also angry with "the white man," the anti-segregationists, for failing to show up at the march.

"I'm ashamed of my race," he said. "The Negroes are brave enough to go out and be arrested by the thousands, but the white man is a coward at this point."

Jewish marchers included survivors of World War II concentration camps.

Carl Allen, Rockwell's deputy, decided to give a speech, even though he did not have the required permit to do so: "We are here to protest by as peaceful means as possible the occupation of Washington by forces deadly to the welfare of our country."

After warning Allen three times, police officers cuffed him and hauled him to jail. Disgusted, Rockwell and his small band of Nazis marched single file across the bridge to Virginia, as far away from the brave Black people as they could get.

In just a few minutes, another march—larger, more powerful, and a rainbow of colors—would begin.

The Ku Klux Klan responded to the march by holding a rally at its birthplace in Georgia, about twenty miles east of Atlanta.

A. Philip Randolph leading the Big Ten through the Capitol Rotunda

18

THE PEOPLE LEAD THE WAY

The people were ready. But where in the world were the leaders?

Earlier in the day, after eating breakfast together, the Big Ten had climbed into three large black limousines for a short trip to the Capitol, where they were scheduled to meet with congressional leaders. Inside the corridors of power, NAACP leader Roy Wilkins—who still preferred the quiet tactic of lobbying—served as the spokesperson.

The meetings proved rough going. Republican Senator Everett Dirksen of Illinois said he would not support the bill if it required the elimination of segregation in places like stores, restaurants, and hotels. That type of requirement would infringe on an owner's right to conduct business as they chose, he claimed.

Democratic House Speaker John McCormack of Massachusetts offered no promises when Walter Reuther pressed for legislation that would raise the minimum wage from $1.25 to $2.00. Nor did McCormack assure the group that their demand for a Fair Employment Practice Committee—a federal agency that would combat discrimination in employment—would make it into a final version of the president's civil rights bill.

The congressional leaders did acknowledge that parts of the bill were passable, but not in the immediate future. For now, the bill was stalled in committees, and the Big Ten could do nothing to pry it loose.

Enough entertainment! Let's march!

At 11:20 a.m., the people couldn't wait a minute longer. So, on their own, without direction, and forty minutes ahead of schedule, they set their sights on the Lincoln Memorial—and began to move.

The march was on!

Bayard Rustin panicked, again.

"My God, they're going," he gasped. "We're supposed to be leading them."

For a moment, Rustin thought about trying to stop the crowd so that the Big Ten could lead the way. "[B]ut I figured I was going to get run over, I'd better get the hell out of there, and I left," he said later.

Emcees Ossie Davis and Ruby Dee weren't sure what to do, but one thing was clear—the people were *unstoppable*!

Davis did the best he could. He used his actor's voice to urge the demonstrators to go to both Constitution Avenue and Independence Avenue, where Black women leaders would lead the way.

There's Jackie Robinson!

David and Jackie Robinson (center) marching with Daisy Bates and Rosa Parks

Jack Roosevelt Robinson—who had cracked the racial barrier in Major League Baseball in 1947—draped his big arm over his son David's shoulder, and together they made a beeline for Independence Avenue.

There, about sixteen people stood abreast in the front line of marchers. Only two in the front were women—Daisy Bates and Rosa Parks.

Bates was in the center. With Robinson now to her right and Rosa Parks to her left, she reached out for their hands and held them tight. Hand in hand, they kicked off their part of the march.

Directly behind them, someone held up an official sign—WE MARCH FOR FIRST CLASS CITIZENSHIP NOW!

After hearing about the early start, the Big Ten scrambled back to their limousines.

"We were supposed to be the leaders," John Lewis recalled. "And it was like [us] saying, 'There go my people; let me catch up with them.'"

The limos headed down Constitution Avenue, but at a snail's pace.

"The crowds were too thick," Lewis said. "We were surrounded by a sea of humanity . . . It was truly awesome, the most incredible thing I'd ever seen in my life."

In some areas, the crowd was so dense that the march was a "slow shuffle," with people moving just a few inches at a time. Thrilled but exasperated, the Big Ten hopped out of the cars, joined hands, and began marching to the Memorial.

"A revolution is *supposed* to be unpredictable," remarked one of King's aides.

Rustin instructed march marshals to clear a space between the leaders and the people ahead of them so that the media could get the pictures they craved. The photographs suggested that the leaders were at the front of the march, but those who were there knew the truth—the *people* were the real leaders.

All kinds of people!

Women in church dresses, girls in jeans. Men in ties, boys in T-shirts. Babies in strollers, older people in wheelchairs. Straight people, LGBTQ+ people. Asian Americans, European Americans. Black people, Brown people. Rich people, poor people. Northerners, Southerners. Easterners, Westerners.

All kinds of people—and all appearing to be heading in one direction. Jean Shepherd felt there was "a feeling of humanity in the air, like we're all in something together."

But there were other feelings, too—lots of them.

A somber group carried a coffin draped with the Confederate flag. "Jim Crow Is Dead," an unofficial sign explained.

Young marchers from Plaquemine, Louisiana—who still suffered from burns inflicted by police officers who had used cattle prods to break up their protest—danced up Constitution Avenue. *Joyfully*!

At 20th Street and Constitution Avenue, Edward Shell, a twenty-year-old white man, charged the marchers, grabbed a protester's sign, and smashed it to pieces.

In another area, strong-minded teens sang, "I'm gonna walk, walk, I'm gonna talk, talk, I'm gonna keep my mind on freedom."

A silent SNCC marcher carried a homemade sign that read, "We Demand an Honest Investigation of the Police Brutality in Southwest Georgia."

And pride—*deep* pride—showed on the faces of folks marching under approved signs and banners that identified their faith communities, civil rights organizations, and labor unions.

At least two hundred domestic workers from New York City—Black women who cleaned the homes of wealthy white people—proudly marched under the banner of the National Domestic and Migrant Workers Association.

In still another section, an older sharecropper from Maryland smiled her biggest smile. "I wouldn't have missed it for the world," she said. "I stopped buying newspapers and saved my pennies, nickels, and dimes so I could come to Washington and march for freedom."

And Chuck Stone, the tough editor of the *Chicago Defender,* cried when he saw a middle-aged Black woman marching with an iron cast on her leg. "Every step was painful, and as she walked, nobody reached out because she didn't want help, nor did she ask for pity. But she marched and dragged that leg and there wasn't a dry eye within yards of her," Stone recalled. "She became my symbol of the Negro Revolution. She understood why she was there."

Alone or in groups, women filled the ranks of marchers.

Anna Arnold Hedgeman was the lead organizer of the thousands of marchers representing the National Council of Churches.

Together, the official signs, colored red and white, and blue and white, represented patriotism and protest.

Puerto Rican Americans were well represented among the marchers.

The fierce resolve of marchers was on full
display for the global audience.

Young marchers showed a wide range of emotions, from righteous anger to sheer joy.

The Big Ten did not make it in time to lead the march, even though some photographs made it seem as if they were at the front.

A reporter with the *New Yorker* observed that "in the march itself there was a remarkable lack of noise. Occasionally, a song would start somewhere in the crowd, but to a large extent the marchers were silent."

Perhaps the people remembered that the Big Ten had called for the march to be "a solemn and dignified tribute" to Medgar Evers, William Moore, Herbert Lee, and thousands of others who had died in pursuit of racial equality. Perhaps they knew, despite the organizers' silence about it, that today was the eighth anniversary of the lynching of fourteen-year-old Emmett Till in Money, Mississippi.

There were no official signs with the names of the dead, but as marchers drew near the Lincoln Memorial, they could see a crude wooden sign displaying a poem honoring Medgar Evers. A stanza that referred to a bloodstained US flag read:

> *Ole Glory's tarnished with his blood*
> *For having shabbily allowed*
> *A noble son to be downtrod*

George Epstein, the organist at the Lincoln Memorial, was supposed to welcome everyone with "We Shall Overcome." But he didn't know how to play it, and the person with his sheet music was stuck in traffic somewhere. While Epstein tried not to panic, a knowledgeable minister quickly scribbled down the notes and placed them on the music holder. With that minor problem solved, Epstein happily played on.

Not everyone sang along, of course.

When Mrs. Greene, an older Black woman, approached the Memorial, she wasn't singing a note. Instead, she was telling the freelance journalist next to her, a white woman named Gloria Steinem, that no women were scheduled to be speakers.

Steinem hadn't noticed.

Where is Ella Baker? Greene demanded. *She trained all those SNCC young people. What about Fannie Lou Hamer? She got beaten up in jail and sterilized in a Mississippi hospital when she went in for something else entirely . . . This is black women's story, from rape to sterilization. Who will speak about that?*

Greene's radical critique impressed Steinem, who in a few years would become a leader of the women's rights movement.

"Not only had I never made any such complaints," Steinem said later, "but at political meetings I had given my suggestions to whatever man was sitting next to me, knowing that if a man offered them, they would be taken more seriously."

A handmade tribute to Medgar Evers

Mrs. Greene then switched to a kinder tone.

You white women, she said, *if you don't stand up for yourselves, how can you stand up for anybody else?*

ELLA BAKER AND FANNIE LOU HAMER

Affectionately referred to as "a whirlwind" for her tireless energy, Ella Baker held leadership positions within the NAACP and the Southern Christian Leadership Conference. She was also the spark behind the creation of the Student Nonviolent Coordinating Committee (SNCC). Both Baker and Fannie Lou Hamer shared a strong belief in grassroots organizing. "Strong people don't need strong leaders," Baker said, suggesting that people who were well organized and committed to a goal didn't need a single recognized leader. Two months before the March on Washington, while working as a SNCC field staffer, Hamer, along with other activists, was arrested and brutally beaten by police in Winona, Mississippi, for challenging segregation in public accommodations.

At this very moment inside the Lincoln Memorial, John Lewis was standing up for all the SNCC workers and allies who had fought so hard for freedom.

A new fight was erupting . . .

MARCH ON WASHINGTON
FOR JOBS AND FREEDOM
AUGUST 28, 1963

LINCOLN MEMORIAL PROGRAM

1. The National Anthem *Led by* Marian Anderson.

2. Invocation The Very Rev. Patrick O'Boyle, *Archbishop of Washington.*

3. Opening Remarks A. Philip Randolph, *Director March on Washington for Jobs and Freedom.*

4. Remarks Dr. Eugene Carson Blake, *Stated Clerk, United Presbyterian Church of the U.S.A.; Vice Chairman, Commission on Race Relations of the National Council of Churches of Christ in America.*

5. Tribute to Negro Women
Fighters for Freedom Mrs. Medgar Evers
    Daisy Bates
    Diane Nash Bevel
    Mrs. Medgar Evers
    Mrs. Herbert Lee
    Rosa Parks
    Gloria Richardson

6. Remarks John Lewis, *National Chairman, Student Nonviolent Coordinating Committee.*

7. Remarks Walter Reuther, *President, United Automobile, Aerospace and Agricultural Implement Wokers of America, AFL-CIO; Chairman, Industrial Union Department, AFL-CIO.*

8. Remarks James Farmer, *National Director, Congress of Racial Equality.*

9. Selection Eva Jessye *Choir*

10. Prayer Rabbi Uri Miller, *President Synagogue Council of America.*

11. Remarks Whitney M. Young, Jr., *Executive Director, National Urban League.*

12. Remarks Mathew Ahmann, *Executive Director, National Catholic Conference for Interracial Justice.*

13. Remarks Roy Wilkins, *Executive Secretary, National Association for the Advancement of Colored People.*

14. Selection Miss Mahalia Jackson

15. Remarks Rabbi Joachim Prinz, *President American Jewish Congress.*

16. Remarks The Rev. Dr. Martin Luther King, Jr., *President, Southern Christian Leadership Conference.*

17. The Pledge A Philip Randolph

18. Benediction Dr. Benjamin E. Mays, *President, Morehouse College.*

"WE SHALL OVERCOME"

The official Lincoln Memorial Program

PART FIVE

THE LINCOLN MEMORIAL PROGRAM

Roy Wilkins, shown here in his NAACP cap, was furious about John Lewis's militant speech.

19

FREEDOM FIGHTERS

As Lewis had been warned the night before, several members of the Big Ten had a big problem with John Lewis's speech—it was too *radical*. They had complained about it during the march, and now, in a room deep inside the Lincoln Memorial, they demanded that Lewis change it.

Wilkins exploded. Shaking an angry finger in Lewis's face, the NAACP head accused Lewis of "double-crossing" the Big Ten's commitment to passing the bill.

How can you not *support this bill wholeheartedly?! That's what we're marching for!*

Wilkins, like other Big Ten leaders, thought the bill was weak—they would say as much in their own speeches—but neither he nor the others were willing to withdraw an ounce of support for the bill.

Lewis shook his finger right back, saying his job was to represent SNCC and their belief that the bill was "too little and too late."

The tension between the men was so high that Rustin had to pull them apart.

Union leader Walter Reuther had been in touch with the Kennedys about Lewis's speech, and they were all peeved. The Kennedy confidant also disliked Lewis's swipe at "cheap political leaders who build their careers on immoral compromises."

Although that was bad enough, the worst part was Lewis's "calling for open revolution," as the union leader put it later. Part of the offensive passage read: "We will take matters into our own hands . . . If any radical, social, political, and economic changes are to take place in our society, the people, the masses, must bring them about."

Reuther urged his Big Ten colleagues to take immediate action.

"If John Lewis feels strongly that he wants to make this speech, he can go someplace else and make it, but he has no right to make it here, because if he tries to make it, he destroys the integrity of our coalition," Reuther said. "This is just immoral . . . and I demand a vote right now because I have got to call the Archbishop."

Archbishop O'Boyle—another close friend of the Kennedys—was holed up in a nearby hotel, still stubbornly refusing to offer the opening prayer. Yes, Lewis had deleted his description of patience as "a dirty and nasty word," but the Catholic leader, like Reuther, was also upset about Lewis's claim that SNCC would use a "scorched earth" policy and burn down Jim Crow throughout the South.

The waiting crowd was unaware of the debate raging behind the massive columns.

The Big Ten voted on the question of whether Lewis should revise his speech. The tally was 9–0 against Lewis, who didn't vote, and Rustin immediately appointed a subcommittee to work out an acceptable solution. Reuther rushed off to call O'Boyle and assure him that everything would be okay.

"We have set up this subcommittee," Reuther explained. "If they agree the speech complies, then John Lewis will make the speech. If they agree it doesn't, he will be denied the floor."

Lewis was livid. He also stood his ground.

Then, A. Philip Randolph—who was every bit as militant as Lewis—turned toward his younger colleague. Lewis thought he looked on the verge of tears.

"John, we've come this far together," Randolph said. "Let us *stay* together."

Lewis loved and respected Randolph too much to say no.

I'll make the changes, Lewis replied.

Without delay, Lewis and SNCC colleague James Forman got to work. Forman sat at a portable typewriter, and Lewis hovered over his shoulder. Both were determined to make as few changes as possible.

"If the church people didn't like it, they could go to hell," Forman thought.

While Forman typed away, another entertainment program was underway on the main platform in front of the Lincoln statue.

Joan Baez, Odetta, and Josh White performed again, and a popular white folk group—Peter, Paul and Mary—sang two favorites among the younger generation: "Blowin' in the Wind" and "If I Had a Hammer."

The Freedom Singers—six young Black vocalists from SNCC—were a crowd favorite. The group's popular lead alto, twenty-two-year-old

Rutha Mae Harris, was already a veteran in the civil rights movement. Before joining the group, she had protested for civil rights in Albany, Georgia.

"We never knew what to expect," she recalled. "We didn't know whether we would get shot or whether we would get beat up."

In those scary moments, the freedom songs gave her strength. "[T]hey kept me from being afraid."

Harris was also arrested and jailed during the Albany protests, and every time the police tried to take her into custody, she made her body limp—a tactic she'd learned in classes on nonviolence.

Now, standing in the shadow of Abraham Lincoln's statue, she led her group in one of her favorite songs—"We Shall Not Be Moved."

MALCOLM AT THE MARCH

Seventeen-year-old Sondra Michelle Barrett—a volunteer marshal—was responsible for crowd control on one city block. Part of her responsibilities included escorting people from her zone to the marshal in charge of the next block. Barrett's assigned area was so far from the march that she couldn't hear the music and speeches as clearly as she'd hoped. Although disappointed, she experienced the thrill of a lifetime when Malcolm X showed up on her block. Barrett was awestruck. "I felt I was in the presence of genius, that I was in the presence of greatness," she said. But she didn't let her feelings detract from her job. Barrett happily escorted Malcolm and his followers to the next block.

Around 1:30 p.m., emcee Ossie Davis introduced a surprise guest—entertainer Josephine Baker.

Dressed in a blue military uniform, Baker basked in the applause.

Josephine Baker in her French Resistance uniform

"I want you to know that this is the happiest day of my life," she enthused.

Older folks in the crowd knew that Baker had survived the East St. Louis Riot of 1917, when white people had burned entire Black neighborhoods and killed hundreds of Black Americans, and that she'd eventually fled to France.

Baker loved her adopted country so much that during World War II she joined the French Resistance and spied on German Nazis. For her brave service, France awarded her a special medal called the Legion of Honor.

Now, at the Memorial, Baker proudly displayed the medal on her French Resistance uniform. She also used her brief speech to add an international dimension to the protest.

"The results today of seeing you all together is a sight for sore eyes," she said. "You're together as salt and pepper just as you should be. Just

*Cooling off in the
Lincoln Memorial
reflecting pool*

as I've always wanted you to be, and peoples of the world have always wanted you to be."

The crowd appreciated the personal touch of Baker's remarks. She wasn't giving a polished speech. It was just Josephine Baker speaking from her heart.

"I want you to know also how proud I am to be here today," she continued. "And after so many long years of struggle fighting here and elsewhere for your rights, our rights, the rights of humanity, the rights of man, I'm glad that you have accepted me to come. I didn't ask you. I didn't have to. I just came because it was my duty, and I'm going to say again you are on the eve of complete victory. Continue on. You can't go wrong. The world is behind you!"

As she finished her short speech, the crowd gave her a polite round of applause.

For Mrs. Greene and Anna Arnold Hedgeman, it was a bittersweet moment. While they welcomed Baker's words, they also knew, and regretted, that this was the one and only time when the crowd would hear a full speech by a woman.

Rita Moreno and Sammy Davis, Jr., right, were part of the celebrity contingent from Hollywood.

20

CELEBRITIES

"I am a Puerto Rican and I want to feel that I speak for my people when I say that I wanted to be here more than anything else in the world," said Rita Moreno.

Two years earlier, Moreno had starred in the film adaptation of an enormously popular Broadway musical—*West Side Story*. The role made her recognizable to millions across the country.

Today, she was part of a multiracial contingent of celebrities who were given choice seats at the Lincoln Memorial. Actor and singer Harry Belafonte had organized their attendance, hoping that their presence would help legitimize the march for everyday people across the country.

When Rita Moreno spoke, people listened, especially the reporters who now gathered around her.

"I support the civil rights bill, but with reservations," she said. "I protest the omission of police brutality in it." Moreno's opinion must have shocked those who weren't used to hearing actors—*especially a Puerto Rican woman!*—speak out about politics. But it must have pleased all the marchers who agreed that the bill was deficient and that it should give the federal government tools for eliminating police brutality and protecting civil rights activists.

Another radical celebrity voice came from Marlon Brando.

The famous Hollywood actor had wanted the celebrities to chain themselves to the Memorial, but moderate voices, particularly actor Charlton Heston's, crushed that idea. But there was no way that Heston could silence Brando's militant words.

Actor Marlon Brando holding a cattle prod to highlight police brutality against civil rights protesters

In his interviews with reporters, Brando compared police officers in Alabama to German Nazis in World War II. The Alabama police, he said, used "indescribable tortures seen previously only in Nazi Germany."

As he spoke, Brando held a cattle prod like the ones that white police officers had used to shock and burn civil rights protesters in Gadsden, Alabama. A reporter asked Brando why he had brought the prod to the Memorial.

"Because there is nothing so symbolic of this spirit of oppression than this—a cattle prodder," the actor replied.

One famous singer, dancer, and actor held back from granting interviews. Instead, Lena Horne encouraged reporters to speak with activists who were on the front line of the civil rights movement.

When SNCC's Joyce Ladner saw Horne on the speakers' platform, Horne gave her a big hug. The two women shared a rich history—both had worked with Medgar Evers.

Just days before Evers was murdered, Horne sang at a civil rights rally organized by Evers in Jackson, Mississippi. Her last selection was "We Shall Overcome," and she invited the audience of three thousand to sing along with her.

After hugging Ladner, Horne arranged for her to be interviewed live by NBC news reporter Nancy Dickerson. Watching the march at home in Mississippi, Ladner's mother couldn't believe it.

That's Joyce!

While celebrities were giving interviews, white folk singer Bob Dylan performed one of the songs he had practiced back in Rachelle Horowitz's apartment.

It wasn't a happy-clappy song. Or a song that called for everyone to come together in a spirit of hope. It was a mournful song about the murder of Medgar Evers.

As Dylan began singing "Only a Pawn in Their Game," every single person behind him was moving, talking, not paying attention. But those who listened to the lyrics heard a radical claim: that a white-controlled political and economic system, rather than individual poor white folks, were ultimately responsible for the racial violence that brutalized and killed Black people. Yes, Byron De La Beckwith was the one who had shot Evers, but the shooter himself was the tool of a murderous *system* that taught poor white people to hate all Black people. Dylan's song was lost on many, but it offered some of the most controversial, and militant, content of the entire entertainment program.

In the room deep inside the Memorial, John Lewis, Jim Forman, and a few members of the Big Ten worked furiously to revise and finish Lewis's speech.

Adopting a gentle approach, Martin Luther King, Jr., commented on the "scorched earth" passage that irritated Archbishop O'Boyle and Walter Reuther.

"John, that doesn't sound like you," King said.

Lewis and Forman agreed, and they cut that part.

The two SNCC leaders also deleted the part that decried the civil rights bill as "too little and too late," as well as the description of politicians as "cheap."

Standing nearby, Rev. Eugene Carson Blake urged Lewis to cut "revolution" and "the masses," saying they sounded like words used by communists. But A. Philip Randolph immediately objected.

"There's nothing wrong with those two words," he said. "I've used them many times myself."

Randolph didn't tell anyone, but in a matter of minutes, he would use those two words in his own speech.

John Lewis, third from left in the back row, faced intense pressure to change the fiery tone of his speech from several members of the Big Ten.

A view of the two
hundred and fifty
thousand marchers
from the steps of the
Lincoln Memorial

21

A SOCIALIST REVOLUTION

The time to start the official program had arrived—*almost*.

"Will Camilla Williams please come to the platform?" asked a march announcer with a bit of desperation in his voice.

The opera star was shocked to hear her name, and she rushed to the main podium.

Marian Anderson is late! someone told her. *Will you please take her place?*

Ever the professional, Williams gathered herself, and on a moment's notice, she began the program with a moving rendition of the national anthem—a difficult feat under the best of circumstances.

Archbishop O'Boyle stood nearby. He had arrived in a limousine shortly after Walter Reuther assured him that John Lewis would change the speech or not deliver it. Now, after all the fuss, it was O'Boyle's turn.

He read a somber prayer.

At long last, A. Philip Randolph walked to the podium for the opening speech.

The massive crowd stretched out before him was not the 100,000 that Rustin months earlier had predicted. It was at least 250,000 strong.

"My fellow Americans," Randolph began. "We're gathered here for the largest demonstration in the history of this nation . . . We are not a mob. We are the advance guard of a massive, moral *revolution* for jobs and freedom."

Randolph was not an electric speaker by any measure. His special gift was to sound dignified while shredding his opponents, and it didn't

A. Philip Randolph served as emcee for the Lincoln Memorial program.

take long before he faulted those who focused only on passing Kennedy's civil rights bill.

The goal of the revolution, he said, was not merely passing a law that desegregated public facilities.

"Yes, we want all public accommodations open to all citizens, but those accommodations will mean little to those who cannot afford to use them."

This echoed the socialist point that he and Rustin had made way back in their December meeting. *What good is a desegregated restaurant if you can't buy a hamburger? To achieve total freedom, Black people must have jobs. And this means that the government must make massive changes to the economy and create full employment.*

"Yes, we want a Fair Employment Practice Act," Randolph continued, "but what good will it do if profit-geared automation destroys the jobs of millions of workers, black and white?"

A United Auto Workers marcher with a sign that mirrored Randolph's message

This, too, referred back to a socialist point that he and Rustin had made. *Capitalist factory owners care more about profits than their workers. To achieve total freedom, Black people must revolt against unfettered capitalism and demand that government protect workers everywhere.*

Next, Randolph denounced the conservative, capitalist argument that people should be free to run their own businesses as they saw fit.

Conservatives who made this point often appealed to a "Mrs. Murphy," a mythical white widow who rented rooms in her home to supplement her low income. *Shouldn't this poor, elderly woman be free to rent her own rooms to whomever she chooses?*

Randolph had an answer. Yes, Mrs. Murphy has property rights, but she does not have the right to discriminate against anyone because of the color of their skin.

"The sanctity of private property takes second place to the sanctity of the human personality."

For Randolph, the "moral revolution" was about toppling white-dominated capitalism and replacing it with a socialist economy that recognized human equality and provided all people with their basic needs—food, shelter, education, health care, and dignity—even if that required sacrificing profits and individual property rights along the way.

Also, in *Randolph's* socialist revolution, *Black* Americans would play the leading role exactly because they had suffered the most under capitalism.

"It falls to the Negro," he declared, "to reassert this proper priority of values [people over profits and property rights], because our ancestors were transformed from human personalities into private property."

Because slavery, with its profit motive, had turned Black people into tools for amassing wealth, it was Black people who truly understood the immorality of capitalism and the need for a socialist economy.

"It falls to us [Black Americans] to demand new forms of social planning, to create full employment, and to put automation at the service of human needs, not at the service of profits," Randolph asserted.

What a historical—and *radical*—moment!

Never had so many people heard a Black American leader lambaste

US capitalism and call for a Black-led revolution that would supplant capitalism with socialism.

And, remarkably, Randolph did all this without ever using the words "capitalism" and "socialism." As a seasoned speaker, he recognized that both were abstract words that could make people glaze over and tune out. Plus, people tended to associate socialism with Russian communism, a dictatorial system that denied fundamental rights, like the right to worship freely. So Randolph simply refused to use either "capitalism" or "socialism."

But anyone who paid close attention to his speech, and knew a bit about capitalism and socialism, would have easily recognized that *Randolph's* march, above all else, was primarily a Black-led socialist march for jobs and economic justice.

And he wasn't done yet.

The dignified labor leader also delivered a swift jab to those who denounced militants in the civil rights movement.

"It was not until the streets and jails of Birmingham were filled that Congress began to think about civil rights legislation," Randolph said.

The crowd cheered at the mention of Birmingham. No doubt, they called to mind the militant students who had engaged in civil disobedience—the tactic that Wilkins had ruled out for today's protest.

"Those who deplore our militants, who exhort patience in the name of a false peace, are in fact supporting segregation and exploitation," Randolph added.

As he concluded, the veteran militant did what radical speakers usually do—he issued a direct threat.

"The months and years ahead will bring new evidence of *masses in motion for freedom* . . . When we leave, it will be to carry . . . the civil rights revolution home with us into every nook and cranny of the land, and we shall return again and again to Washington in ever-growing numbers until total freedom is ours."

Randolph might have *sounded* aristocratic, but the content of his words revealed that the elder statesman of the civil rights movement was a fierce Black militant calling for an open revolt against Washington's political and economic establishment.

Members of Congress arriving after Randolph's opening speech

Having set a militant tone for the march, Randolph then turned to the next order of business—welcoming members of Congress.

About one hundred members smiled and waved as they walked down the steps of the Memorial to the reserved seats below. They planned to stay for about fifteen minutes before heading back to the Capitol for a pending vote.

Some members lingered in front of the television cameras for an extra second of coverage, but none dared to stop at the speakers' podium. They had *not* been invited to speak. They had been invited to attend, sit among the people, listen to speakers above them, and hear the people's demands for jobs and freedom now. This was the "new concept of lobbying" that Rustin had planned.

And then, something dramatic happened that even Rustin had not predicted. As the politicians smiled and waved, the marchers began to shout, "Pass the bill! Pass the bill! Pass the bill!"

It was a loud demand, not a quiet request, and the members of Congress weren't sure what to make of it. They weren't used to being treated this way. But if they hadn't recognized it earlier, they certainly understood it now: Today, the *radical masses* were in charge.

STROM THURMOND SPEAKS OUT

In its televised coverage, NBC broadcast a pre-taped interview with Strom Thurmond, the segregationist senator from South Carolina. Thurmond said he was concerned that the march might suggest to other countries that Black Americans "don't have freedom over here." They do, he said. "Our Negroes own more refrigerators than in any other country in the world." What do you think about Thurmond's comments? Was the ownership of refrigerators and cars an indicator of Black freedom? Thurmond also said this about Black people in search of work: "[I]f they're qualified they can always get jobs." Can you identify any problems with Thurmond's claim?

Gloria Richardson, left, a civil rights leader from Cambridge, Maryland; Dr. Rosa L. Gragg of the National Association of Colored Women's Clubs; and Diane Nash Bevel, right, of the Southern Christian Leadership Committee, speaking with the press after a meeting at the White House on July 9, 1963

22

A TRIBUTE TO BLACK WOMEN

Back in Birmingham, Alabama, Diane Nash Bevel watched the march on a television in her hotel room. It was a special treat.

She and her husband, James, had worked day and night to recruit Birmingham folks for the march. After making sure everyone was safely aboard the buses, James turned to her and said: "Diane, you know, with everybody having left and gone to Washington, we could get some rest if we stayed here."

The suggestion was music to her ears, and the two checked into a Birmingham hotel for some well-deserved time off. Settled in their room, they ordered food and enjoyed the march.

While the people were still yelling at the members of Congress, demanding that they pass the civil rights bill, A. Philip Randolph introduced a "Tribute to Negro Women, Fighters for Freedom."

Diane sat up and paid close attention.

"Fellow Americans," Randolph said, "in great tribute to the role the Negro woman has played in the cause of freedom, equality, and human dignity, I now call on Miss Daisy Bates, that great champion of Negro rights and freedom, to give awards to Diane Nash Bevel, Mrs. Herbert Lee, Rosa Parks, and Miss Gloria Richardson."

Diane was shocked.

No one had told her that she would be honored.

CAMPING ON THE WHITE HOUSE LAWN

In the spring of 1963, Diane Nash Bevel and her then-husband James Bevel talked about holding "a national camp-out on the White House lawn" to "solidify and insist on" the goals of the civil rights movement. The idea of a protest camp wasn't brand new; in 1932, US military veterans had camped in Washington, DC, to demand payment of a "bonus" for their service in World War I. But the idea was still exciting, and Nash Bevel held a few strategy sessions about it, including one attended by Martin Luther King, Jr. The encampment idea never gained any traction, and Nash Bevel eventually abandoned it. But what do you think about it? Would it have worked? Would it have been more militant or more effective than the march?

Daisy Bates wasn't the Big Ten's first choice to present the awards. The men wanted to reserve that honor for Myrlie Evers, but by the time they invited her, she had already committed to a speaking engagement in Boston.

Later, Evers thought that was probably for the best, given the mix of emotions she felt after her husband's murder. "I was hurt; I was very, very angry," she recalled. "I was dealing with a split personality—one that said, 'Move forward; don't hold the anger within,' and the other part of me said, 'Vengeance will be mine.'"

Taking Evers's place, Bates strode to the microphone with her typical confidence and flair. But instead of giving awards, she read a short statement penned by a man, John Morsell, an NAACP staffer assigned to work on the march.

"Mr. Randolph," Bates said, "the women of this country pledge to

Daisy Bates also addressed the crowd at the Washington Monument.

you . . . to Martin Luther King, to Roy Wilkins, and all of you fighting for civil liberties, that we will join hands with you, as women of this country."

Though Bates read the statement with conviction, the words must have rung hollow to the honorees, as well as countless others, who well knew that women were courageous *leaders*, not merely supportive *partners*, in the civil rights movement.

Bates herself was a fierce leader, but if she was frustrated by the words she was reading, she gave no indication. Her voice was crystal clear.

"We will kneel-in, we will sit-in, until we can eat in any corner in the United States," she continued. "We will walk until we are free, until we can walk to any school and take our children to any school in the United States. And we will sit-in, and we will kneel-in, we will lie-in, if necessary, until every Negro in America can vote. This we pledge you."

After reading the statement, Bates was supposed to introduce the honorees, but for some reason, Randolph returned to the podium and retook control of the tribute.

"May I request the women we are honoring to stand," he said. "Mrs. Diane Nash Bevel of the Student Nonviolent Coordinating Committee; Mrs. Herbert Lee, the wife whose husband was killed in Mississippi two years ago, because he tried to register to vote; Mrs. Medgar Evers, widow of the NAACP . . ."

Hearing the reference to Myrlie Evers, the crowd erupted, giving her their loudest cheer yet. As marchers craned their necks to catch a glimpse of her, Randolph corrected himself.

"I'm sorry to report to you that Sister Evers could not attend our demonstration because of, uh, unusual circumstances."

Then, Randolph forgot the names of the other honorees.

Richardson was known for her militant leadership of the civil rights movement in Cambridge, on the eastern shore of Maryland.

"Who else?" he stumbled.

Bayard Rustin announced the names from behind him, but Randolph still struggled.

"Will the . . . Miss Rosa Parks," he said in an unsure voice. "Will they all stand? And Mrs. Gloria Richardson."

Against her better judgment, Richardson was wearing a denim skirt. The tough SNCC activist usually dressed in jeans and a blouse, just in case she ended up in jail, but a march organizer had asked her to dress up for the occasion.

Richardson was also "seething inside," as she put it, because someone had taken her reserved seat at the start of the program. "You should raise hell," Josephine Baker told her, but Richardson thought better of it.

Now, though, Richardson was excited. An organizer had informed her that she would have two minutes to address the crowd, and she planned to use every second of it.

Her bold plan was to encourage the 250,000 marchers to carry out civil disobedience—to "sit here until this no-good [civil rights bill] passes." Like John Lewis, Richardson thought that the bill was terribly weak, but she also thought that passing it was important enough to warrant massive sit-ins—and *right now!*

But the organizer was wrong. Richardson was not offered a chance to speak. Rosa Parks and Prince Lee didn't have a chance, either, and Diane Nash Bevel was more than seven hundred miles away. Richardson was furious.

As the tribute ended, Anna Arnold Hedgeman and her women colleagues on the platform looked at one another in dismay.

More than anyone else, they recognized the awful irony of the moment—that even while the Big Ten were calling for first-class citizenship for all Black Americans, they were also treating Black women as second-class citizens.

Rosa Parks—who had launched the careers of several men sitting near her—turned to Daisy Bates with the assurance that "our time will someday come."

But Dorothy Height, the president of the National Council of Negro Women, had more concrete action in mind. That night, she and other Black women would gather to talk about their experiences at the march. They would also begin to devise a strategy for fighting the painful bias against women in the civil rights movement.

But first, another man made his way to the podium.

23

A MINISTER CONFESSES, MARIAN ANDERSON RETURNS

About thirty thousand white Protestants were among the marchers, and most of them had been recruited, directly or indirectly, by Anna Arnold Hedgeman. A leader in the National Council of Churches (NCC) had asked her to round up that many, and she had succeeded.

But Hedgeman wasn't invited to speak on behalf of the NCC or all the people she had enlisted to march. That prominent role fell to a white man on the NCC's Commission on Religion and Race—Reverend Eugene Carson Blake.

The "Protestant Pope," as some called him, began his speech by observing that the racial crisis existed "partially because the churches of America have failed to put their own houses in order."

He was certainly right about that. The Christian church—Protestant, Catholic, and Orthodox—was one of the most segregated institutions in the United States, and white Christians were late arrivals to the civil rights movement.

"We come, and late we come," Blake confessed.

Although he didn't explain this, the white minister was drawing from his own personal experiences. Blake had participated in his first civil rights demonstration only *two months* before the march. Protesting at an all-white amusement park in Maryland, he'd been arrested and thrown in jail.

*Reverend Eugene Carson Blake, right, was a
newcomer to the civil rights movement.*

"The churches in this country have for a long time been saying a great deal about discrimination," he said at the time. "Almost all the churches have made the right statements, but we can no longer let the burden of winning freedom for the Negro or any other oppressed people be the burden only of the oppressed people themselves."

He added, "Churchgoers should stop regarding God as a white, American idol."

Although some praised Blake for his brand-new activism, others faulted him for being a traitor to his race and religion.

"I am delighted to learn that you are in jail," a church member wrote. "If we could keep you there it would be a boon to Christianity."

Freed from jail, the square-jawed minister now praised those who had led the way before him—his Black colleagues in the Big Ten, "these

*Black Baptist ministers played major roles in
local and national campaigns for civil rights.*

amazingly able leaders of the Negro-Americans, who to the shame of
almost every white American have alone and without us mirrored the
suffering of the cross of Jesus Christ."

Blake's rather bland speaking style belied the power of his words.
This marked the first time that millions of Black Americans heard a
humbled white minister of national importance publicly confess that
the white church had failed to treat Black people with love, dignity, and
respect. For Black folks, this was a moment of unadorned truth.

As Blake ended his short speech, some marchers replied with the word that seemed most fitting—"*Amen!*"

Marian Anderson arrived at the Lincoln Memorial in tears. The world-renowned contralto was distraught that she had missed her chance to sing the national anthem.

While Randolph comforted her, Rustin cleared a space in the program. Anderson was *that* important—to the march, the marchers, and US history.

On Easter Sunday in 1939, Anderson had stood before a crowd of seventy-five thousand people, about half of them Black Americans, at this very same location. They had come not only to hear her beautiful voice but also to protest the Daughters of the American Revolution, an all-white organization, for having denied her the opportunity to sing at a concert venue they owned—Constitution Hall, located near the White House, just a few blocks from the Lincoln Memorial.

At the start of her program, the dignified Anderson took a deep breath, closed her eyes, and began with a lyric near and dear to her heart: "My country, 'tis of thee, sweet land of liberty."

Her rich voice regaled not only the crowd but also millions of people tuned in on their radios at home, including ten-year-old Martin Luther King, Jr., in Atlanta.

After Anderson sang her last selection, the crowd was so moved that they cheered until she quieted them with an encore—"Nobody Knows the Trouble I've Seen." Given the troubles she had faced, the Black spiritual felt like the perfect conclusion to her recital.

Anderson's 1939 concert at the Lincoln Memorial was one of the

Marian Anderson performing at
the Lincoln Memorial in 1939

Anderson's voice had aged by 1963, but her performance at the march was still breathtaking.

greatest demonstrations for civil rights in US history. It also established an enduring symbol for Black people. From that moment on, the Memorial became the most significant national symbol of protest for Black civil rights.

Now, twenty-four years later, Anderson was back.

Despite her historic role in the movement, she was not known for speaking out about racial injustice or joining street protests for civil rights.

"I'm not marching, just singing," she'd told reporters just before the march. And for her, that was good enough. Anderson believed that the best way she could contribute to the civil rights movement was through her music.

"We would like to do for you a Negro spiritual which has been a favorite of many audiences throughout the United States," she announced to the crowd at the Memorial.

"Come on!" an encouraging voice shouted.

Anderson then delivered an emotionally powerful rendition of "He's Got the Whole World in His Hands." Her contralto voice, aged but still strong, sought to comfort and soothe the crowd with the assurance that God was in control. A few marchers locked arms in solidarity. Others closed their eyes. Nearby, a young mother sang along, pulling her two sons close.

But inside the Memorial, John Lewis prepared to roar!

THE SEGREGATED OPENING OF THE LINCOLN MEMORIAL

On May 30, 1922, the government held a ceremony marking the official dedication of the Lincoln Memorial. Black attendees were horrified to learn that attendance at the event was racially segregated and that white speakers downplayed Lincoln's historic decision to issue the Emancipation Proclamation. Former President William Howard Taft totally ignored the topic of slavery, emphasizing national unity instead, and President Warren G. Harding stated that Lincoln "would have been the last man in the republic" to go to war to free the slaves. Only Robert Russa Moton, the Black president of the Tuskegee Institute, dared to declare that Lincoln's greatness lay in his decision to speak "the word that gave freedom to a race and vindicated the honor of a Nation conceived in liberty and dedicated to the proposition that all men are created equal."

President Warren Harding speaking at the 1922 dedication of the Lincoln Memorial

Black newspapers criticized the event. The *Chicago Defender* wrote, "The venomous snake of segregation reared its head at this dedication. At a memorial to the Great Emancipator!" The newspaper also declared that although the memorial was now open to the public, "it remains undedicated," tarnished by white politicians who had defiled Lincoln's legacy. Sounding even more defiant, the *Defender* called upon its readers to boycott the memorial, to stay away from it, until a time when people who believed in justice held power. "With song, prayer, bold and truthful speech, with faith in God and country, later on let us dedicate the temple thus far only opened," wrote the *Defender*. For many Black Americans, that moment arrived seventeen years later, when Marian Anderson gave her historic recital.

Many commentators believed that John Lewis delivered the most militant speech of the day.

24

LEWIS SCORCHES

The Department of Justice was ready.

Inside the Lincoln Memorial, a DOJ staffer was poised to turn off the sound system. His instructions were simple: If a speaker called for violence, or a riot broke out, flip the kill switch.

The staffer was in communication with law enforcement sources planted among the marchers—DC police officers, FBI agents, and Army intelligence personnel in civilian clothing. He was also in touch with officials at command centers based at the DOJ and the Pentagon.

Of special concern to everyone was the next speaker.

"Brother John Lewis!" announced A. Philip Randolph.

"The sound of applause was immense," Lewis recalled.

He was so nervous his body trembled. Glimpsing at the massive crowd, he licked his lips, which were dried out from nervousness and the heat. He wasn't sure he'd be able to speak, but to his right, he could hear a SNCC group cheering him on.

For them, this was the highlight of the day. Earlier, they had talked about everything they considered wrong about the march—its praise for the civil rights bill, the absence of civil disobedience, and all those marchers who "had not done a damn thing for civil rights," as Jim Forman put it. The SNCC group also believed that the march squandered precious resources.

But now, in this moment, the SNCC team set aside their complaints and cheered their leader.

"We march today for jobs and freedom, but we have nothing to be proud of," Lewis began, "for hundreds and thousands of our brothers are not here, for they are receiving starvation wages, or no wages at all."

The SNCC crowd nodded their heads. They had pressed organizers for funds so that poor people in the South could attend the march. But the bulk of those funds never came through, and most poor folks were left to listen to the march on radios back home—if they were lucky enough to be off work and near a radio.

"It is true that we support the administration's civil rights bill," Lewis continued. "We support it with great reservations, however."

Lewis had agreed to take out his description of the bill as "too little and too late," but he had never promised to refrain from criticizing it.

Lewis was arrested at least forty times during the civil rights era.

And now he took aim at the bill's failure to include "Title III," which would allow the Department of Justice to file civil rights suits in cases of police brutality.

"Unless Title III is put in this bill," Lewis said, "there's nothing to protect the young children and old women who must face police dogs and fire hoses in the South while they engage in peaceful demonstration."

Nor would the bill protect "the citizens of Danville, Virginia, who must live in constant fear of a police state" or "the hundreds and thousands of people that have been arrested on trumped-up charges."

Lewis was in his groove.

"The crowd was with me, hanging on every word, and I could feel that," he said later. And he loved the call-and-response—the way he made a forceful point and the crowd responded with positive encouragement.

Come on, John! Tell it!

The cheering freed him to express his righteous anger. "The speech itself felt like an act of protest to me," he recalled. "It felt like defiance." Defiance of Archbishop O'Boyle. And Walter Reuther. And Reverend Blake. Defiance of the Kennedys. And the Justice Department. Defiance of brutal police officers. And segregationists. And racism everywhere.

"As it stands now," Lewis continued, "the voting section of this bill will not help the thousands of Black people who want to vote."

Yes! That's right!

SNCC workers had long focused on voter registration so that Black people could rise up, throw racists out of office, and govern themselves. And the activists were irate about a proposed section of the bill that seemed to require voters to have at least a sixth-grade education. Some Black citizens in the Deep South didn't even know how to sign their name.

"'One man, one vote' is the African cry," Lewis thundered. "It is ours, too. It must be ours."

The crowd cheered and applauded.

Supportive SNCC colleagues applauded the militancy of Lewis's speech.

"We need a bill that will provide for the homeless and starving people of this nation," Lewis rolled on.

"We need a bill that will ensure the equality of a maid who earns $5.00 a week in a home of a family whose total income is $100,000 a year."

The capitalists in the crowd must have been horrified by these words. *Equality between a poor maid and her wealthy employer would require a socialist revolution!*

Domestic workers were among the lowest paid in the US labor force.

"My friends," Lewis added, "let us not forget that we are involved in a serious social *revolution*."

Tell it, John!

Yes, Lewis had agreed not to call politicians "cheap," but he had not promised to let them off the hook. And now he delivered a powerful uppercut to the jaws of politicians in both major parties, Republicans and Democrats.

"By and large, American politics is dominated by politicians who build their career on immoral compromises and align themselves with open forms of political, economic and social exploitation."

Yes!

"Where is *our* party? Where is the political party that will make it unnecessary to march on Washington?"

That's right! Where?

And yes, Lewis had agreed to remove his description of patience as "a dirty and nasty word," but he had not promised to get rid of his attack on calls for patience.

"To those who have said, 'Be patient and wait,' we must say that we cannot be patient. We do not want our freedom gradually, but we want to be free now!"

That's right! Now!

Lewis said the revolution of 1776 was not yet complete for Black Americans. This was true, despite the role that Black Americans like Crispus Attucks, an American sailor of African and Indigenous descent and one of the first colonists to die in the fight for liberty at the Boston Massacre in 1770, played in that revolution.

"We are tired. We are tired of being beaten by policemen. We are tired of seeing our people locked up in jail over and over again, and then you holler, 'Be patient.' How long can we be patient? We want our freedom and we want it now!"

Now!

Then Lewis spoke directly to his audience, using the two words that Eugene Carson Blake had criticized—"revolution" and "masses."

"I appeal to all of you to get into this great revolution that is sweeping this nation," Lewis urged. "Get in and stay in the streets of every city, every village and hamlet of this nation until true freedom comes, until the revolution of 1776 is complete."

Some marchers probably raised their eyebrows at this point. *The 1776 revolution? Wasn't that a violent uprising?* Lewis didn't explain; for now, he just let the point hang there.

"We must get in this revolution and complete the revolution. In the Delta of Mississippi, in southwest Georgia, in the Black Belt of Alabama, in Harlem, in Chicago, Detroit, Philadelphia, and all over this nation, the black masses are on the march for jobs and freedom."

The Black masses! No one else, not even A. Philip Randolph, had dared to use such radical language.

As he concluded, the twenty-three-year-old militant issued a direct threat, just as Randolph had done. And while Lewis did not include the "scorched earth" language, he made sure that his threat packed a punch.

"We will not stop," Lewis boomed. "If we do not get meaningful legislation out of this Congress, the time will come when we will not confine our marching to Washington. We will march through the South, through the streets of Jackson, through the streets of Danville, through the streets of Cambridge, through the streets of Birmingham."

Lewis was on such a roll now that he didn't even stop for the resounding applause.

"But we will march with the spirit of love and with the spirit of dignity that we have shown here today.

"By the force of our demands, our determination, and our numbers, we shall splinter the segregated South into a thousand pieces and put them together in the image of God and democracy.

"We must say, 'Wake up, America. *Wake up!*' For we *will* not and *cannot* be patient."

The SNCC leader quickly gathered his papers, and for a moment, the crowd seemed stuck in a state of mild confusion. *Did he just finish? Is it over?* But they quickly showered him with praise.

As he walked away, Lewis noticed that all the hands reaching out to shake his were black. Not one white person—neither Reuther nor Blake nor O'Boyle—offered him their hand.

A. Philip Randolph returned to the podium, and for the first time in the program, a slight smile appeared on his face as he prepared to introduce the next speaker.

THE FIREWORKS CONTINUE

After John Lewis, a number of gifted orators addressed the crowd, as the program built toward the final speech of the day by Martin Luther King, Jr., and the closing pledge by A. Philip Randolph.

WALTER REUTHER, President, United Automobile, Aerospace and Agricultural Implement Workers of America, AFL-CIO; Chairman, Industrial Union Department, AFL-CIO:

"President Kennedy has offered a comprehensive but moderate

bill. That bill is the first meaningful step. It needs to be strengthened . . . And the job question is crucial, because we will not solve education or housing or public accommodations as long as millions of Americans, Negroes, are treated as second-class economic citizens and denied jobs. And as one American, I take the position [that] if we can have full employment and full production for the negative ends of war, then why can't we have a job for every American in the pursuit of peace?"

JAMES FARMER (read by Floyd McKissick), National Director, Congress of Racial Equality:

"Some of us may die like William L. Moore or Medgar Evers, but our war is for life, not for death. And we will not stop our demand for our freedom now . . .

"We will not come off of the streets until we can work at a job befitting of our skills in any place in the land. We will not stop our marching feet until our kids have enough to eat and their minds can study a wide range without being cramped in Jim Crow schools.

"Until we live wherever we choose, and can eat and play with no closed doors blocking our way . . . We will not stop until the heavy weight of centuries of oppression is removed from our backs and, like proud men everywhere, when we can stand tall together again."

RABBI URI MILLER, President, Synagogue Council of America:

"Above all, we pray we become cognizant in ever-increasing measure that our religious ideals must be fulfilled in actual living experience. Our traditions must be given flesh in the form of social justice now. Freedom, pride, and dignity must not be empty words, nor even sincere ideals projected into some messianic future, but actualities expressed in our society in concrete and tangible form now."

WHITNEY M. YOUNG, JR., Executive Director, National Urban League:

"Furthermore, we must work together even more closely back home where the job must be done to see that Negro Americans are accepted as first-class citizens and that they are enabled to do some more marching.

"They must march from the rat-infested, overcrowded ghettos to decent, wholesome, unrestricted, residential areas . . .

"They must march from the relief rolls to the established retraining centers. From underemployment as unskilled workers to higher occupations commensurate with our skills.

"They must march from the cemeteries where our young and our newborns die three times sooner and our parents die seven years earlier. They must march from there to established health and welfare centers.

"They must march from the congested, ill-equipped schools, which breed dropouts and which smother motivation, to the well-equipped integrated facilities throughout the city."

MATHEW AHMANN, Executive Director, National Catholic Conference for Interracial Justice:

"Who can call himself a man, say he is created by God, and at the same time take part in a system of segregation which destroys the livelihood, citizenship, family life, and very heart of the Negro citizens of the United States of America? Who can call himself a man and take part in a system of segregation which frightens the white man into denying what he knows to be right, into denying the law of his God?"

ROY WILKINS, Executive Secretary, National Association for the Advancement of Colored People:

"All over this land and especially in parts of the Deep South, we are beaten, kicked, maltreated, shot, and killed by local and state law enforcement officers. It is simply incomprehensible to us here today, and to millions of others far from this spot, that the United States government, which can regulate the contents of a pill, apparently is powerless to prevent the physical abuse of citizens within its own borders . . . Now, the president's proposals represent so moderate an approach that if it is weakened or eliminated, the remainder will be little more than sugar water. Indeed, as it stands today, the package needs strengthening. And the president should join us in fighting to be sure that we get something more than pap."

Mahalia Jackson was King's favorite gospel singer.

25

MAHALIA JACKSON MOVES THE SEA

Lula Patterson's male editor gave her an unsurprising assignment: "Do a color job on the women . . . how they look . . . how they dress."

It took about a minute for the *Afro-American* reporter to see that the march was "no high dress affair." The event was a "working march," and many women wore simple dresses or pants, cotton shirts, and flats.

Patterson also noticed that some of the women on the speakers' platform were in formal attire. "Rosa Gragg, head of the National Association of Colored Women, dressed to the nines in pale blue silk, a white turban with drapes to the side," she observed.

But when Mahalia Jackson—the Queen of Gospel—took center stage, Patterson lost her reporter's focus.

"And that Mahalia Jackson! That Mahalia! Her fine black jacket dress, lined with yellow and black print and worn with a blouse of the same print, was a nice item. But *who looked* as she enthralled them with the singing of 'I've Been 'Buked and I've Been Scorned' at [the] request of Dr. Martin Luther King."

Indeed! Who looked?

King and Jackson had first met when she performed at a fundraiser for the Montgomery bus boycott, and ever since then they had stayed in touch. They were so close that when King felt downhearted, he would call her on the phone, and she would sing him a comforting gospel song. At other times, she would cook for him.

King's request for today was a mournful spiritual, a soulful callback to all the pain that Black people had suffered because of slavery, Jim Crow, and racism.

Jackson began the spiritual slowly, drawing out the words to emphasize just how long Black people had been rebuked and scorned.

"Iiii've been 'buuuuked."

Then, with her whole body gently swaying, she put her head down.

"And Iiii've been scorrrrned."

A remarkable stillness descended on the massive crowd. Some marchers no doubt wondered how Jackson had been rebuked and scorned. *Did white people call her awful names? Did they refuse to serve her in stores and restaurants and hotels? Did they threaten her life? Did they make fun of her for being a large Black woman with little formal education?* Yes, all that was true.

Other marchers called to mind their own trials and tribulations. An older Black woman bowed her head, and a younger one covered her mouth. Perhaps they had been slapped and beaten. Or raped. Perhaps they had seen their mothers and daughters, and fathers and brothers, sobbing in secret.

The pain ran deep, and by the time Jackson finished, tears were flowing everywhere.

New York State Senator James L. Watson—who had earned the Purple Heart military decoration while fighting with segregated Black troops in World War II—turned to the reporter next to him and said: "I just have to cry a little."

Mahalia Jackson had moved this sea of humanity.

The Queen of Gospel returned to her seat, but the crowd wouldn't let her stay there. For her encore, Jackson chose "How I Got Over," a rollicking spiritual about surviving—and conquering—oppression.

Many in the crowd smiled and laughed and shouted joyfully. Women waved their handkerchiefs, and children tried to clap in time with the fast rhythm.

Jackson sang with so much enthusiasm that a nurse feared the singer was having some sort of seizure. "Do you think she needs first aid . . . is she all right?" the nurse asked a reporter.

Her voice raspy and forceful, Jackson finished with a loud shout—"*Hallelujah!*"

"I wish I could sing," said Rabbi Joachim Prinz, the speaker who followed Jackson.

The crowd laughed, but the German rabbi didn't linger in the humorous moment. Like Jackson, Prinz had a difficult past he wanted to share—a past that in some ways paralleled Black history in the United States.

"Our ancient history began with slavery and the yearning for freedom," he said, referring to Jewish people. "During the Middle Ages, my people lived for a thousand years in the ghettos of Europe." And because of this experience, Jewish people could identify and empathize with Black Americans.

The rabbi also recalled his own painful past. In Nazi Germany, he had spoken out against Hitler's regime, and the Nazis despised him for it. The Gestapo—Hitler's secret police force—harassed and arrested him numerous times before expelling him in 1937. That awful experience of antisemitism left Prinz with a powerful lesson.

"The most important thing I learned in my life and under those tragic circumstances was that bigotry and hatred are not the most urgent problem. The most urgent, the most disgraceful, the most shameful, and the most tragic problem is silence."

Prinz lamented that Germany had become a "nation of silent onlookers" during brutal Hitler's reign of hatred, terror, and mass murder.

Using an urgent tone, the rabbi insisted that America must not be like Germany. "America must not remain silent . . . It must speak up and act, from the president down to the humblest of us, and not for the sake of the Negro, not for the sake of the black community, but for the sake of the image, the idea, and the aspiration of America itself."

Little did Prinz know, but in just a few moments, "the aspiration of America itself" would reach new heights in the soaring dream of Martin Luther King, Jr.

26

THE DREAM

"At this time, I have the honor to present to you the moral leader of our nation," announced A. Philip Randolph.

That simple declaration was yet another subversive act. Randolph, after all, was implying that the moral leader of the United States was *not* President John F. Kennedy. Or FBI Director J. Edgar Hoover. Or Senator Strom Thurmond. Or Archbishop Patrick O'Boyle. Or Reverend Eugene Carson Blake. Or anyone else in the nation.

The title of "moral leader" belonged to one person alone—*the Rev. Dr. Martin Luther King, Jr.*

Martin Luther King, Jr., evoked Lincoln's signing of the Emancipation Proclamation in 1863.

King received the compliment with a slight smile and a nod to the cheering crowd. They had waited all day for this moment.

With his eyes focused on the written text, King began by declaring that the march was the most important protest for freedom in US history.

King spoke slowly, almost haltingly, and his voice sounded serious and determined as he recounted President Lincoln's signing of the Emancipation Proclamation in 1863. "But one hundred years later," King added, "the Negro still is not free."

"My Lord," said Mahalia Jackson, seated nearby.

Mahalia Jackson, foreground, urged King to share the dream that she had heard him recount in an earlier speech in Detroit.

The call-and-response that John Lewis had experienced during his speech was back, and this time it had the distinct feel of a church service. The minister preached, and the flock responded.

"[T]he life of the Negro is still sadly crippled by the manacles of segregation and the chains of discrimination," King said.

Yes!

He was speaking a bit faster now.

Afro-American reporter Lula Patterson found herself distracted from King's message by "the beauty of his oratory." A young man next to her was also awestruck. "He handles words as if he invented them," the man said.

But it was more than King's language that was impressive. It was the way he moved with his words, and modulated his voice, and used his hands, and kept a beat that echoed the hearts of his audience.

"He's damn good," said President Kennedy in the Oval Office.

HOW DID HE DO THAT?

Dr. King and his advisers worked on his speech well in advance of the march, but his written text did not include any mention of his now-famous dream. Many people still marvel at King's ability to deliver extemporaneous remarks. But did his dream really come to him in the moment? Did he make it up right then and there? Not exactly. King often memorized and used refrains, anchored by texts and phrases, that he had given in earlier speeches. In fact, he had delivered his "I have a dream" refrain on June 23, 1963, in a speech at the Detroit Walk to Freedom, and before then, he had used it during the Birmingham campaign in April. On August 28, as he felt the crowd moving with him, King sensed that sharing his dream yet again would be the best way to inspire everyone

> to fight for racial equality and live up to the nation's democratic ideals. Although the dream sounded refreshing and brand-new to his listeners, it was already deeply entrenched in King's heart and mind.

Then, like John Lewis, King denounced police brutality, and like A. Philip Randolph, he criticized economic injustice and praised the "new militancy" erupting in Black communities.

But King also added something different—the perspective of a loving parent. As the father of four children, he often referred to young people in his speeches. Today, he did the same. "We can never be satisfied," he said, "as long as our children are stripped of their selfhood and robbed of their dignity by signs stating 'for whites only.'"

Like Prinz before him, the moral leader spoke from personal experience.

When he was fourteen years old, King had won an oratorical contest in Dublin, Georgia, with a speech titled "The Negro and the Constitution." His stirring words claimed that US democracy was deficient because of the nation's unfair treatment of Black people.

Young King was overjoyed, but on the trip home, a white bus driver ordered him and Sarah Grace Bradley, one of his favorite teachers, to surrender their seats to white people boarding the bus. The driver even cursed King and Bradley for not moving fast enough.

"I intended to stay right in that seat," King said later, "but Mrs. Bradley urged me up, saying we had to respect the law. We stood up in the aisle for ninety miles to Atlanta."

King had never felt angrier. The driver and the white passengers had destroyed the joy he felt about his award. But worse, they had stripped him of his selfhood and robbed him of his dignity.

"Let us not wallow," King now said.

The crowd was right there with him, urging and encouraging him to lead them to a place beyond despair.

King looked up from his prepared remarks. Feeling the crowd's rising hopes, he realized that this was no time to continue reading his speech. It was time to speak from his heart, to let the crowd carry him upward, and to soar with his people.

"I still have a dream," King said.

"Dream on!" someone shouted.

Resounding cheers rolled toward him from below, and King looked up to the sky as he shared his dream.

"I have a dream that my four little children will one day live in a nation where they will not be judged by the color of their skin but by the content of their character."

"I see it!" someone yelled as King dreamed on.

Edith Lee-Payne, who turned twelve on March Day, did not know about this photo until she was forty-seven years old.

His moving words struck a chord with thirteen-year-old Sharon Robinson, the daughter of Jack and Rachel Robinson. They took her back to her painful elementary school days when her classmates thought her brown skin was dirt. But Sharon didn't wallow in the memory. Inspired by King, she dreamed, right then and there, of the right to speak up for herself—to *be* herself.

"I have a dream," King continued, "that one day in Alabama . . . little black boys and black girls will be able to join hands with little white boys and white girls as sisters and brothers."

King was on fire!

As he concluded his speech, he clenched his fists and raised his hands.

"When we allow freedom [to] ring . . . we will be able to join hands and sing . . . *Free at last! Free at last! Thank God Almighty, we are free at last!*"

The crowd thundered!

For many, King's dream marked the emotional high point of the day.

They laughed. They cried. They hugged. They waved. They jumped up and down. They fell on their knees.

Even SNCC workers were ecstatic!

"We were on our feet, laughing, shouting, slapping palms, hugging, and not an eye was dry," SNCC worker Michael Thelwell said later.

The *masses* were on fire!

They'd just heard—they'd just *experienced*—one of the greatest speeches of US history.

THE THREE LIVES OF THE DREAM SPEECH

In the aftermath of the march, Dr. King's speech was widely heralded as the highlight of the day both for its delivery and its content. King's ability to frame the hopes and aspirations of the civil rights movement, especially in a tone appealing to white liberals, earned high praise.

But in the months and years after the march, many people soured on the man and his message. Within the civil rights movement, militants criticized King's dream as wistful and fanciful, an abject failure to recognize the intransigence, or stubbornness, of racism. Positive feelings toward King and his speech also faded as he began to criticize poverty and US involvement in the Vietnam War. In 1968, the year of his assassination, a poll showed that King had a public disapproval rating of nearly 75 percent.

But then another shift happened. After King's assassination, white political leaders believed that Black militants would spark violent rebellions across the country. Fearing Black uprisings, white leaders began to praise King and his dream once again, hoping that Black people would follow his peaceful example rather than calls for a violent revolution. In the hands of white politicians, King's dream became a tool to keep Black people orderly and peaceful. Further, as they lauded King's dream of racial harmony, white leaders ignored his harsh criticisms of economic injustice and war; in effect, they reduced King to his dream.

Today, Dr. King is widely regarded for his peaceful leadership of the civil rights movement and its calls for racial integration. A recent poll, for instance, found that 95 percent of respondents considered King to be one of the most important figures in US history. Still, most people see and know him primarily through the narrow lens of his iconic speech.

27

WE DEMAND

Poor Patricia Worthy! The receptionist from march headquarters in New York had fallen asleep. She was so tired from answering all those calls, and from the heat of the day, that she had dozed off during King's dream. But now she was as awake as the electrified crowd.

After the applause finally died down, A. Philip Randolph returned to the podium with a special announcement: "I want to introduce now Brother Bayard Rustin, who will read the demands of the March on Washington Movement."

It was another subversive protest! An act in direct defiance of Senator Strom Thurmond. And Robert Kennedy. And all those who had ridiculed Rustin, or sought to keep him in the background, because of his homosexuality and his radical politics.

"Everyone must listen to these demands," Randolph announced. "This is why we are here."

Randolph's words urged everyone to remember that the march was more than a dream. It was a *demand*. A *radical* demand. A demand for *jobs*. A demand for *freedom*. A demand for jobs and freedom *now*!

As Randolph stepped aside, Bayard Rustin—the gay, pacifist, socialist ex-convict who had been pushed aside so many times in his life—took control of the podium. His tie was loose, and he looked frazzled, perhaps because all afternoon he had buzzed about like a stage director, making sure the speakers and musicians were prepared, in the right places, and on schedule. But now it was finally his turn to be in the spotlight.

Only a few people knew in advance that Rustin would deliver the demands of the march. His name was not listed in the official program.

"Friends," he announced, "at five o'clock today, the leaders whom you have heard will go to President Kennedy to carry the demands of this *revolution!*"

Yeah!

"It is now time for you to act. I will read each demand, and you will respond to it, so that when Mr. Wilkins and Dr. King and the other eight leaders go [meet with President Kennedy], they are carrying with them the demands which you have given your approval to."

Rustin's words helped everyone understand that this was a *people's revolution!*

"The first demand," Rustin shouted, "is that we have effective civil rights legislation, no compromise, no filibuster, and that it include public accommodations, decent housing, integrated education, and the right to vote. What do you say?"

Still hyped from King's dream, the people shouted.

Yes! We demand!

"We demand that segregation be ended in every school district in the year 1963."

Yes! The roar for this demand was absolutely deafening. No one, not even Patricia Worthy, could have slept through it.

Rustin continued.

"We demand that every person, black or white, be given training and work with dignity to defeat unemployment and automation."

We demand!

Enjoying every second of this moment, Rustin punctuated his words by thrusting his right fist into the air. The gesture echoed the fist of solidarity that socialists had long raised while marching for workers' rights.

"We demand an increase in the national minimum wage so that men may live in dignity."

We demand!

PIONEERS IN THE GAY AND LESBIAN RIGHTS MOVEMENT

Seven members of the Mattachine Society of Washington (MSW)—a gay and lesbian rights group founded in 1961—attended the march. Although they marched as a group, they did not carry signs identifying themselves or their group's purposes. "We reasoned that it would be impolite," recalled cofounder Jack Nichols. But as King gave his inspiring speech, Nichols imagined that MSW and its allies would one day march for gay and lesbian rights. Less than two years later, on April 17, 1965, Nichols and nine others, including Lilli Vincenz, the first lesbian member of MSW, picketed the White House. It was the first organized march on Washington by a homosexual rights organization.

Jack Nichols, Frank Kameny, and Lilli Vincenz leading a 1965 march for gay and lesbian rights

After Rustin finished the demands, one major item remained on the official program.

"And now, ladies and gentlemen, Mr. Randolph will read the pledge," Rustin announced. "This is a pledge which says our job has just begun. You pledge to return home to carry out *the revolution!*"

Randolph returned to the podium. He looked tired, but this was it—the last of his responsibilities at the Lincoln Memorial.

"*The pledge!*" Randolph said in his authoritative voice.

Inviting everyone to stand, the march director read the marchers' pledge. It ended with a fervent commitment: "I pledge my heart and my mind and my body, unequivocally and without regard to personal sacrifice, to the achievement of social peace through social justice."

PLEDGE Standing before the Lincoln Memorial on the 28th of August, in the Centennial Year of Emancipation, I affirm my complete personal commitment to the struggle for Jobs and Freedom for all Americans.

To fulfill that commitment, I pledge that I will not relax until victory is won.

I pledge that I will join and support all actions undertaken in good faith in accord with the time-honored democratic tradition of non-violent protest, of peaceful assembly and petition, and of redress through the courts and the legislative process.

I pledge to carry the message of the March to my friends and neighbors back home and to arouse them to an equal commitment and an equal effort. I will march and I will write letters. I will demonstrate and I will vote. I will work to make sure that my voice and those of my brothers ring clear and determined from every corner of our land.

I pledge my heart and my mind and my body, unequivocally and without regard to personal sacrifice, to the achievement of social peace through social justice.

NAME_____

ADDRESS_____
_____
(Street and number or R.D. Box number)

_____ Date:_____1963
(City or town)   (Zone)   (State)

252

The pledge recited by marchers near
the end of the program

Rustin approached the microphone for the last time.

"How do you pledge?" he shouted to the crowd.

In one thunderous voice, the people replied.

"I do pledge!"

The Rev. Dr. Benjamin Mays—who had taught Martin Luther King, Jr., when he was a student at Morehouse College—stepped forth to offer the benediction, the closing prayer.

"Here we are, God," Mays prayed, "one hundred eighty million people, one hundred years after Lincoln freed the slaves, ninety-eight years after the close of a bloody civil war, fought to preserve one nation under God, indivisible, one hundred eighty-seven years after Jefferson declared that all men are created equal, that they are endowed by their Creator with certain inalienable rights, that among these are life, liberty, and the pursuit of happiness.

"Here we are God, confused, baffled, floundering, afraid, faithless,

debating whether the Congress of the United States should pass legislation guaranteeing to every American the equal protection of the
law, debating whether its business should have the right to discriminate
against a man because thou, oh God, made him black.

*Rev. Dr. Benjamin Mays wearing a lei sent
by march supporters in Hawaii*

"In peace and in war, thou hast blessed America. As the nations of
the earth look to the United States for moral and democratic leadership, may we not fail them, nor thee. Please, God, in this moment of
crisis and indecision, give the United States wisdom, give her courage,
give her faith to meet the challenge of this hour. Guide, teach, sustain,
and bless the United States, and help the weary travelers to overcome,
someday soon. Amen."

As the official program concluded, the organist played "We Shall
Overcome."

At the foot of the Memorial, a group of march staffers, SNCC workers, and everyday people crossed their arms, linked their hands, and sang along.

Most folks started to return to the buses and trains and cars, but some stood still, reflecting on the day.

Randolph's Dream Comes True

By ETHEL L. PAYNE

It seems impossible that it was 22 years ago when the dream of a March on Washington was first born; but there was the record in the pages of a scrap book, the leaves so brittle that they crumbled at the slightest touch.

In one of my rare seizures of orderliness, I spent a quiet weekend just digging through mounds of papers and pamphlets in that old wooden file which I have been trying to tidy up for the past three years. When I came across the book, my efforts ceased as I became lost in memories.

June 6, 1942 — Letter from A. Philip Randolph to the City-Wide Committee March on Washington Movement, Chicago. "Our parade in New York was a tremendous success.

I hope your parade in Chicago will be big and enthusiastic. Here are some things to do:

1. Make the parade an overwhelming success.

2. Put a placard in every place where Negroes gather.

3. Have some stickers made with: '50,000 Negroes Must Attend the Coliseum Mass Meeting to Fight Jim Crow Friday, June 26th, 7 p.m.' At the bottom put: 'Winning Democracy for the Negro Is Winning the War for Democracy.' . . .

4. "Get the church choirs if possible for singing. Don't have them sing any spirituals unless it is 'Joshua Fit the Battle of Jericho.' "We don't want any songs of resignation, but pieces like 'A Mighty Fortress Is Our God.' 'Hold the Fort.' "Onward Christian Soldiers,' 'Battle Hymn of the Republic,' etc. . ."

Signs appear all over the South Side in places of business saying: "We will Be Dark, Dry and Silent During the Coliseum Protest Meeting June 26, 1942."

June 27, 1942 — editorial in the Chicago Defender said: "The mass meeting called for

Friday, June 26 under the auspices of the March on Washington Committee is not meant to intimidate or browbeat constituted authorities.

It is not meant to further depress the morale of the Negro people by disparaging patriotic efforts and desirable enthusiasm.

Nor is it meant to obstruct the National Government program for victory. It is intended on the contrary to arouse our people to a consciousness of their sacred obligation to the Nation — to American Democracy in this hour of gravest peril.

"The crisis of the moment makes it imperative that Negroes demonstrate their collective strength in an unswerving determination to participate in this world struggle. . ."

A columnist for an Eastern paper took a negative view of the whole business. He asked: "If Mr. Randolph organizes the discontented among us, just what is he going to do with them? . . . Last year, Mr. Randolph was made the spearhead of a movement which threatened to fill the nation's capital with thousands of protesting Negroes demanding from their government redress of their grievances.

The movement won some distinction, not because of any inherent usefulness it possessed but rather because the President and Mrs. Roosevelt became alarmed and asked that Washington be spared such a march . . . Cultivation of the Negro's discontent is bound to yield a harvest, but what kind?"

The following week, the Chicago Defender bannered its report on the rally with the Stars and Stripes, saying: '12,000 in Chicago Voice Demands for Democracy." The story said that thousands overflowed into the streets.

What was the harvest which the gloomy writer asked about? Well, it was a partial payment on the demands and

now 22 years later, the man whose dream of a March on Washington was deferred by a promise while a whole new generation of Americans grew up, will at long last lead his legions numbering more than 200,000 across the Potomac and up to the Shrine of the Great Emancipator to demand payment in full on the promissory note.

Walter White who was with him on that first crusade is gone, but Martin Luther King Jr. who was a boy in knee pants then, will be marching abreast with him. The ranks will be swelled with a cross section of Americans of all races, creeds and occupations who now realize that the time has come to fulfill the dream.

A. PHILLIP RANDOLPH.

and Roosevelt Phillips, Neva Ryan, Clementine McConico, Jeska Flemister and Zenobia White, and Frances Matlock.

And there were those adorable kids, Andrew Jarrell, Norvelle West and Rosine Tyler, Otis Boykin and Mary Harris. We worked and we worked. We walked and talked, distributed thousands of leaflets. Whenever "the Chief" (Randolph) would come to town.

I will be watching the panorama with nostalgic remembrance of things past. I was

one of the earnest crusaders trooping starry-eyed behind the Randolph banner. We were in quest of the holy grail and he was our Sir Galahad, a knight in shining armor. We had no money, but some impressive titles — (I was Chairman of the Planning Committee) and lots of fervor.

Old photographs are absorbing and always bring the inevitable question. Wonder where they are now? The stalwarts included Frieda Scott, David and Annabelle Eason, Bill McClaskey, Ted Brown, Maceo Mercer and Charles Burton, Lucille Henderson, Henry Bennett, Esther we would sit and quench our thirsty souls with his eloquent words.

Yes, those were the good old days — they weren't really good days. It just felt good to be a part of the flowing stream of Negro consciousness.

Well, I'm old enough to look back and young enough to climb more mountains in search of the dream. It is good to be alive to witness the honors which will at long last come to the man who for years was a voice crying to the wilderness.

He was a giant in the land. He still is and long after the last footfall has died away from the march, his indelible imprint upon the history of our times will linger on.

Journalist Ethel Payne described the march as the fulfillment of Randolph's longtime dream for racial justice.

It meant a lot.

"Today I am proud to have a black skin," said a college student.

The *Atlanta Daily World* described this palpable sense of pride as the "feeling that on this day, 100 years after their ancestors ceased to be slaves, American Negroes had finally begun to hold their heads high and to walk like free men."

The *Afro-American* put it this way: "If there were tears in the eyes of strong men, they did not weep because of sadness. If they wept it was because the colored people of this nation have come of age, they have grown up, they have gotten off their knees, and now they stand tall and proud."

Inspiring and ennobling, the March on Washington for Jobs and Freedom had also just become the largest and most important nonviolent protest for civil rights in US history. Whether it would create jobs and help pass the civil rights bill remained to be seen, but the 250,000 marchers had already made history.

The historic moment was not lost on the march director or his deputy. Rustin walked over to his mentor after spotting him standing alone near the edge of the Memorial.

"Mr. Randolph, it seems that your dream has come true," Rustin said.

Randolph didn't reply, but the tears streaming down his face said it all. His people—*the masses*—had fulfilled his dream of a radical march.

And better yet, the masses were marching on.

As evening arrives, a bus is ready to carry marchers home.

*Dr. King gifted this pocket watch
to Bayard Rustin to thank
him for his superb and speedy
organization of the march.*

EXTRA STEPS

Here are some fascinating facts not mentioned in our story.

Before March Day

- March headquarters in Harlem received numerous bomb threats and death threats.
- The US Department of the Interior sought to dissuade organizers from holding the rally at the Lincoln Memorial, partly because they thought it would interfere with tourists.
- The *Atlanta Daily World*—the largest Black newspaper in Martin Luther King, Jr.'s hometown—opposed the march and warned about the potential for violence.
- Bayard Rustin squashed a proposal to invite President Kennedy to speak at the march.
- King delivered an early version of his "I Have a Dream" speech at Detroit's "Walk to Freedom," a civil rights march and rally attended by 125,000 protesters.
- FBI agents telephoned celebrities, alleging communist influence in the march and encouraging them to boycott it.
- A plane carrying Robert M. Shelton, the Imperial Grand Wizard and Grand Dragon of the Ku Klux Klan, crashed near Walhalla, South Carolina. Shelton—who was on his way to the march—suffered a broken arm. The pilot died.
- A mail-in campaign asked people unable to attend the march to flood Congress with letters demanding passage of the civil rights bill.

- Eighty-two-year-old Jay Mardo rode his bike from New York City to Philadelphia, where he then hitched a bus ride to the march.
- Members of Hawaii's International Longshore and Warehouse Union sent the march orchid leis—symbols of love, respect, and appreciation.

On March Day

- The temperature was in the low 80s, and humidity hovered around 70 percent.
- Chicago residents who supported the march drove with their headlights on all day, an unusual act in 1963.
- In Cleveland, supporters flew the US flag.
- In Los Angeles, activists marched on City Hall.
- Marchers arriving at Union Station in Washington were greeted by members of the Nation of Islam selling copies of *Muhammad Speaks*, the Nation's newspaper.
- A march announcer asked Governor Ross Barnett of Mississippi to report to the entertainment stage. The joke was a big hit with the crowd.
- There was a bomb scare at the Washington Monument around 1 p.m.
- It took about thirty minutes to march the 0.8 miles from the Monument to the Memorial.
- It took about three hours for the 250,000 marchers to gather at the Memorial.
- Black people comprised about 70 percent of the crowd.
- Many grassroots activists wore denim bib overalls nicknamed "freedom uniforms."
- One marcher carried an unofficial sign that read, "Ban the Bomb Too."

- An informal survey revealed that most marchers were concerned about job opportunities and school integration.
- About 2,000 reporters and photographers covered the march.
- CBS televised the Lincoln Memorial program, and thanks to the new satellite Telstar, the march was broadcast around the world.
- In his prayer, Rabbi Uri Miller quoted a letter that President George Washington had written to the Hebrew Congregation in Newport, Rhode Island, on August 18, 1790. Washington's words are within the single quotes of this part of Miller's prayer: "May we demonstrate our gratitude for the blessed privilege of living under the Stars and Stripes by giving 'to bigotry no sanction, to persecution no assistance.'"
- Thousands of marchers left for home before King shared his dream.
- The march marshals standing behind King wore white paper caps as a tribute to Mohandas Gandhi and his nonviolent protests for a free India.
- CORE founder James Farmer watched the march on a small television in his jail cell.
- Red Cross stations treated more than 1,000 people; many suffered from dehydration, heat exhaustion, and insect bites.
- Not one marcher was arrested.
- There was no violence.
- Rustin estimated that the cost of the march was $125,000.
- After the rally, the Big Ten visited with President Kennedy in the White House. To King, the president said: "I have a dream." To John Lewis, he said: "I heard you speak."
- In the Oval Office, A. Philip Randolph asked for a glass of milk.
- After the meeting, President Kennedy declared that "the cause of 20 million has been advanced."

- Tass, the Soviet Union's news agency, said that the march revealed "the sores of American society" by showing "the repulsive picture of racial oppression and exploitation of 20,000,000 American Negroes."
- On the trip home, four buses carrying marchers were struck by rocks on Route 40 in Maryland.
- But weary marchers continued to sing freedom songs!

THINGS TO CONSIDER

1. Why are mass demonstrations important? Why do you think the leaders of the march elected to march on Washington? Are mass marches more effective than smaller ones?

2. The March on Washington was billed as a March for Jobs and Freedom. However, the organizers sought to highlight other issues as part of the demonstration. If there were a march on Washington today, what issues, relative to racial equality, do you think it might highlight?

3. Several people who spoke at the march shared dreams for racial equality. Why are dreams important? Why is it important to share those dreams? What are some things that you dream about changing or improving in your community?

4. Music played a big part in the civil rights movement and the march. Why do you think the music of the movement was so important?

5. Many people made great sacrifices to participate in the movement and the march. Are there any issues that you feel strongly about that you would be willing to do the same for?

6. As you think about the various individuals and groups who helped to shape the march, who do you think was the most important? The most overlooked or underrated? Can you think of creative ways to highlight and share the contributions of the folks who are largely forgotten?

7. Bayard Rustin found himself frozen out of the movement because of his sexuality, and yet he ended up playing a critical role in the

march's success. What can his story teach us about the importance of not discriminating against others and valuing the participation of all people?

8. Despite the important role played by women in the civil rights movement, the organizers of the march kept them in the background. Do you think that this was fair or unfair? Why?

9. What was the most surprising thing you learned about the origins of the march?

10. How did the organizers demonstrate cooperation and collaboration? Do you think the march could have been successful without these traits?

11. If you could sit down and talk with anyone who participated in the march, what would you ask them? Make a list of three questions that still intrigue you about the march and those who participated.

12. Historical milestones, like the 100th anniversary of the Emancipation Proclamation, and physical spaces, like the Lincoln Memorial, played a big part in the planning of the march. What does this say about the importance of learning and understanding our history? What does it tell us about the importance of commemorating that history, in various forms, as a means of not only documenting the past but inspiring people to imagine a better future?

13. Imagine sitting on the lawn of the Lincoln Memorial surrounded by thousands of other demonstrators listening to the rhythmic flow of Dr. King's powerful speech. What do you find most impactful or inspiring about the speech? Does it enhance or reinforce anything you learned while reading this book? Why do you believe the speech has had such staying power?

14. Besides Martin Luther King, Jr.'s iconic "I Have a Dream" speech, which do you think was the most important or inspiring speech of the day? Why?

15. Ordinary people from across the nation journeyed to Washington to take part in the march. Imagine that you are one of those planning to attend. What will you put in your knapsack? Who are you most excited to hear speak? What issues are you most concerned with?

16. Speeches were the focal point of the Lincoln Memorial program. Imagine that you've recently been invited to give a speech offering the perspective of a young person on a social justice issue. Which issue would you emphasize? Write a 2–3 minute speech that you might give.

ACKNOWLEDGMENTS

Young readers often ask whether we like writing books. The short answer is, *Yes*!

We loved writing this book. It was fun to find long-buried facts, arrange them in the right order, and share them with care and precision. It was also enjoyable to work with all the people who helped us create the book. Just as Bayard Rustin relied on staffers and volunteers to organize the march, we depended on numerous folks to write about it. We're grateful to everyone.

Thanks to all the librarians who helped us with research, especially those at the Free Library of Philadelphia, the New York Public Library, and the Library of Congress in Washington, DC. Bayard Rustin's papers—his speeches, articles, and interviews—are located at the Library of Congress, and we hope you can look at them someday.

Also, be sure to check out a great book by William P. Jones—*The March on Washington*. We're grateful to Professor Jones for his pioneering work on the radical roots of the march.

Our agents, Joan Brookbank and John Rudolph, are amazing. They cheered the book early on and expertly addressed all the dizzying details of business matters.

We've said it before, and we'll say it again: Wesley Adams is a brilliant editor. He's also the Bayard Rustin of this book. Along with his team, he shaped all the words and images so they would leave a lasting impact on our young readers. What a leader!

It's also been wonderful to work with editorial assistant Hannah Miller, whose nuanced perspective and sharp eye for detail strengthened the manuscript.

The excellence of the Macmillan Children's Publishing Group is unmatched. Many thanks to production editor Helen Seachrist, designers Mallory Grigg and Maria W. Jenson, managing editor Allyson Floridia, production manager John Nora, copyeditor Linda Minton, proofreaders Jackie Dever and Edmund Mander, and indexer Elizabeth Parson. Together, they've made this book gorgeous. We're also grateful to publicist Morgan Rath and her enthusiastic resolve to march the book into the world.

Our family and friends deserve special thanks for supporting our march toward publication. Yohuru thanks Alexandra Alves, Ella Williams, Blaire Rodenbiker, and Brynn Kimel. Mike thanks Karin Long, Walter Naegle, Sharon Herr, and Shea Tuttle.

Finally, we thank our readers for their interest in learning about the history and legacy of the march. May each of you march forward with a commitment to racial equality, economic justice, and nonviolence.

Onward!

NOTES

1 / A March for Jobs

5 "promised to look": Lucy G. Barber, *Marching on Washington: The Forging of an American Political Tradition* (Berkeley and Los Angeles: University of California Press, 2002), 112.

5–6 "I suggest that 10,000 Negroes" and "wake up and shock": A. Philip Randolph, "'Let's March on Capital,' Urges Labor Union Head," *Philadelphia Tribune*, January 23, 1941.

6–7 "There shall be no discrimination": "Executive Order," Executive Orders, 1862–2011, General Records of the United States Government, Record Group 11, National Archives Building, Washington, DC; and "Executive Order 8802: Prohibition of Discrimination in the Defense Industry (1941)," archives.gov.

7 "great forward step": "'Postponed,'" *Pittsburgh Courier*, July 5, 1941.

7–9 "the biggest crisis": "Randolph Calls Employment Bias Biggest Crisis," *Atlanta Daily World*, March 28, 1962.

11 "Says 'March on Washington' May Be Necessary to Protest Unequal Negro Employment" *Lewiston Journal* [Maine], February 7, 1962.

2 / A March for Jobs—and Freedom

13–14 "The one hundred years," "two-day action program," and "a mass descent": Untitled document, no date [January 1963], personal papers from the Estate of Bayard Rustin. We thank Walter Naegle for providing us with a copy of this document.

15 "Mister Randolph": Walter Naegle, in conversation with Michael G. Long, New York City, 2012.

16 "pilgrimage" and "unemployment crisis": "Plan D.C. 'Pilgrimage' to Reveal Jobless Crisis," *Chicago Daily Defender*, February 26, 1963.

16 "And that march": "Randolph Warns of Negro Job Loss Due to Automation," *New York Amsterdam News*, March 23, 1963.

16 "a call for an emancipation march": "Job Protest March Slated," *Afro-American*, March 30, 1963.

17 "D-Day": *Mighty Times: The Children's March*, HBO documentary, produced and directed by Robert Hudson, 2004.

17 "We poured into Sixteenth Street": *Mighty Times*, 2004.

19 "We are at the point": David J. Garrow, *Bearing the Cross: Martin Luther King, Jr., and the Southern Christian Leadership Conference* (New York: William Morrow, 1999), 265.

19–20 "for the development": "Labor Leaders Plan March on Capital," *New Journal and Guide* (Norfolk, VA), May 18, 1963.

20   "a march on Washington": "Dr. King Denounces President on Rights," *New York Times*, June 10, 1963.

20   "thousands upon thousands" and "massive acts": "Massive Protest in Capital Seen if Congress Fails to Aid Negroes," *New York Times*, June 12, 1963.

20   "all Americans the right" and "Like our soldiers": "Transcript of the President's Address," *New York Times*, June 12, 1963.

21   "100,000 or more Negroes": "Negro March on Capitol Is Scheduled for August," *New York Times*, June 22, 1963.

21   "There will be job riots": "U.S. Faces Racial Crisis," *New York Amsterdam News*, June 22, 1963.

3 / Kennedy Resists

24   "It was mind-blowing": John Lewis with Michael D'Orso, *Walking with the Wind: A Memoir of the Movement* (New York: Simon & Schuster, 1998), 206.

24   "We want success": Garrow, *Bearing the Cross*, 271.

24–25   "Mr. President, the Negroes": Jervis Anderson, *A Philip Randolph: A Biographical Portrait* (New York: Harcourt Brace Jovanovich, 1972), 326.

25   "There *will* be a march": Taylor Branch, *Parting the Waters: America in the King Years— 1954–1963* (New York: Simon & Schuster, 1988), 840.

25   "To get the votes we need": Garrow, *Bearing the Cross*, 272.

25   "the traditional American way": Marjorie Hunter, "Negroes Inform Kennedy of Plan for New Protests," *New York Times*, June 23, 1963.

25   "could serve as a means": Garrow, *Bearing the Cross*, 272.

27   "We made it clear": Hunter, "Negroes Inform Kennedy of Plan for New Protests," June 23, 1963.

27   "That little baby": Thomas Gentile, *March on Washington: August 28, 1963* (Washington, DC: New Day Publications, 1983), 39.

27   "I favored the quiet": Roy Wilkins with Tom Mathews, *Standing Fast: The Autobiography of Roy Wilkins* (New York: Da Capo Press, 1994), 291.

4 / Choosing the Director

30   "Look, Bayard" and "There are several reasons": Taylor, *Parting the Waters*, 846.

30–31   "I know, I know": Taylor, *Parting the Waters*, 846–847.

31–32   "You can take": Taylor, *Parting the Waters*, 848.

33   "This demonstration is": "Proposed Plans for March," memorandum to James Farmer, Martin Luther King, John Lewis, A. Philip Randolph, Roy Wilkins, Whitney Young, July 2, 1963, Civil Rights Movement Archive (online), https://www.crmvet.org /docs/6307_mow_proposedplans.pdf.

34   "the strongest action": "'Biggest Yet' March on Washington, August 28," *New Journal and Guide*, July 6, 1963.

34   "300,000 TO MARCH ON CAPITAL": "300,000 to March on capital Aug. 28," *Chicago Daily Defender*, July 3, 1963.

5 / Remembering Medgar Evers

38   "Daddy!": Claude Sitton, "Whites Alarmed," *New York Times*, June 13, 1963.

38   "Sit me up": Sitton, "Whites Alarmed," June 13, 1963.

40   "Uncle Tom" and "Jackson must go!": "Mayor, Baptist Leader Shouted Down at Rally," *Call and Post* (Cleveland, OH), July 13, 1963.

40   "Kill him!": M. S. Handler, "Chicago Negroes Boo Mayor Daley," *New York Times*, July 5, 1963.

40   "The parade will dramatize": *March on Washington for Jobs and Freedom, August 28, 1963—Organizing Manual No. 1*, no date [July 1963], 5, https://www.si.edu/object/march-washington-jobs-and-freedom-organizing-manual-no-1%3Anmaahc_2010.45.2.

6 / Visualizing the Day

45   "Where is this young" and "I want to meet": David Matthews and James Polk, "5 Faces from the March on Washington," CNN.com, August 25, 2013.

46   "How could I possibly" and "You are *compulsive*": Milwaukee PBS, "For Jobs and Freedom: 50 Years Later—Rachelle Horowitz," YouTube.com, August 26, 2013, https://www.youtube.com/watch?v=LQh6E-FbxUY.

47–48   "Joyce, Medgar has been killed": "Dorie Ladner and Joyce Ladner Oral History Interview Conducted by Joseph Mosnier in Washington, D.C., 2011 September 20," Library of Congress, https://www.loc.gov/item/2015669153/.

49   "If you want to organize": Branch, *Parting the Waters*, 873.

49   "Toilets were a major": Lewis with D'Orso, *Walking with the Wind*, 217–218.

51   "I wanted to go to sleep": "Dorie Ladner and Joyce Ladner Oral History," September 20, 2011.

51   "could be the spark": "Riot Is Feared," *New York Times*, July 15, 1963.

7 / Kennedy Caves

53   "We will have," "If they march," "white army," and "oppose": Ken Mink, "Marion Talks Set," *Bristol Virginia-Tennessean*, July 12, 1963.

53   "When such an unspeakable" and other quotations from pamphlet: Bruce Phillips, "American Nazis," *Ottawa Citizen*, July 9, 1963.

54 "caused by unorganized," "quite brutal police," and "If these factors": Charles Euchner, *Nobody Turn Me Around: A People's History of the 1963 March on Washington* (Boston: Beacon Press, 2010), 59. We are indebted to Euchner's book for helping us set this scene.

54 "How are you going": Euchner, *Nobody Turn Me Around*, 61.

54 "in excess of 2,000": Rodney H. Clurman to Charles Horsky, memorandum, July 11, 1963, John F. Kennedy Presidential Library and Museum, Boston, Massachusetts. See document at Stacey Flores Chandler, "Making the March on Washington, August 28, 1963," August 27, 2020, https://jfk.blogs.archives.gov/2020/08/27/making-the-march-on-washington/.

55 "there would be no dogs": Clurman to Horsky, memorandum, July 11, 1963.

55–56 "Your job is to see" and "Use every manner": "Keep 100,000 in Order March Marshals Told," *Chicago Daily Defender*, August 15, 1963.

57 "Do you find," "No," "the police," and "I'll look forward": "Transcript of the President's News Conference on Foreign and Domestic Matters," *New York Times*, July 18, 1963.

8 / Malcolm X Speaks Out

59 "Oh, Bayard": Gary Younge, "The Rev. King Didn't Dream of Better People; He Dreamed of a Better System," *Guardian*, August 28, 2013.

59 "The White House absolutely": David Matthews, "Kennedy White House Had Jitters Ahead of 1963 March on Washington," CNN.com, August 28, 2013.

59–60 "What you have to understand": Gary Younge, "Bayard Rustin: The Gay Black Pacifist at the Heart of the March on Washington," *Guardian*, August 23, 2013.

60–62 "The March on Washington projects," "But in keeping," "Instead, we have," "Our demonstration," and "new—and more profound": *Final Plans for the March on Washington for Jobs and Freedom, August 28, 1963—Organizing Manual No. 2*," no date [August 1963], Civil Rights Movement Archive (online), https://www.crmvet.org/docs/moworg2.pdf.

62 "a people's revolution": "'A People's Revolution'—Randolph," *New York Amsterdam News*, July 20, 1963.

62 "much larger than expected": Martin Arnold, "Rights March on Washington Reported Growing," *New York Times*, August 4, 1963.

63 "And time is running out": Malcolm Nash, "Are Negro Groups Lagging Behind?" *New York Amsterdam News*, August 17, 1963.

63 "Up to this time," "The record on," and "The Medgar Evers assassination": Martin Luther King, Jr., "March on Washington," *New York Amsterdam News*, August 24, 1963.

64–65 "unity meeting" and "found out he couldn't": "Church to Enlist Catholics Here for Capital Civil Rights Rally," *New York Times*, August 11, 1963.

65 "The march is a farce," "There will be more," and "I'll be in Washington": Nash, "Are Negro Groups Lagging Behind?" August 17, 1963.

9 / The FBI Attacks

67–68   "I was sentenced to 60 days": Junius Griffin, "Rustin, 'Mr. March,' Has Been Arrested Many Times," *Nashville Banner*, August 8, 1963. An excerpt of Griffin's interview appeared earlier in "King Aide to Tell of Conviction on Morals Charge in California," *Nashville Banner*, August 2, 1963.

68   "No, Mr. Rustin": "March Leader Won't Quit," *Nashville Banner*, August 3, 1963.

68   "If Rustin is Mr. March-on-Washington" and "It is terrible": Frank Van Der Linden, "Thurmond 'Shocked' by Prison Record of March Director," *Nashville Banner*, August 5, 1963.

68   "Communist ideological dogma": "Thurmond Claims 'Whitewash Job' on March Director," *Atlanta Daily World*, August 15, 1963.

68–70   "was arrested for" and "sex perversion": "Sen. Thurmond Charges Washington Post with Distorted, Slanted Reporting About Rustin," *Greenville News*, August 14, 1963. The phrase "sex perversion" is a quotation of the newspaper's description of Thurmond's charges; the phrase, or a close variation of it, appeared in other newspapers.

70   "FBI records": "March Director Whitewashed—Strom," *Charlotte Observer*, August 14, 1963.

70   "abilities and achievements": M. S. Handler, "Negro Rally Aide Rebuts Senator," *New York Times*, August 16, 1963.

70–71   "I am sure I speak," "Twenty-two arrests," "That Mr. Rustin," and "I am dismayed": Handler, "Negro Rally Aide Rebuts Senator," August 16, 1963.

71   "And that was that": John D'Emilio, *Lost Prophet: The Life and Times of Bayard Rustin* (New York: The Free Press, 2003), 349.

10 / The Women Demand

73   "Women are included": Dorothy I. Height, "'We Wanted the Voice of a Woman to Be Heard': Black Women and the 1963 March on Washington," in *Sisters in the Struggle: African American Women in the Civil Rights-Black Power Movement*, eds. Bettye Collier-Thomas and V. P. Franklin (New York: New York University Press, 2001), 85 (digital edition).

73   "We knew, firsthand": Height, "'We Wanted the Voice of a Woman,'" 86.

74   "without causing serious problems": Gentile, *March on Washington*, 141.

75   "We have Mahalia," "But she is not," and "I've never seen": Height, "'We Wanted the Voice of a Woman,'" 87.

75   "all women," "better prepared," and "the young feminist": "Job Problems Facing Race Women Discussed at Hampton," *Atlanta Daily World*, May 14, 1941.

76–77 "In light of the role," "Since the 'Big Six,'" and "That a Negro Woman": Anna Arnold Hedgeman, *The Trumpet Sounds: A Memoir of Negro Leadership* (New York: Holt, Rinehart and Winston, 1966), 179.

77 "No one can quarrel": Hedgeman, *The Trumpet Sounds*, 180.

78 "Tribute to Negro Women": This is the title listed in "The March on Washington for Jobs and Freedom, August 28, 1963—Lincoln Memorial Program," https://www.archives.gov/milestone-documents/official-program-for-the-march-on-washington.

79 "It is ludicrous": "Randolph Is Charged with Bias to Press," *Atlanta Daily World*, August 30, 1963.

79 "can only be construed" and "Frankly, if I were": Pauli Murray, letter to A. Philip Randolph, August 21, 1963, in Lynne Olson, *Freedom's Daughters: The Unsung Heroines of the Civil Rights Movement from 1830 to 1970* (New York: Touchstone, 2001), 288.

81 "It's a hectic time" and "It would be uncivil": "Randolph Is Charged with Bias to the Press," August 30, 1963.

81 "Negro women were accorded": Pauli Murray, *Song in a Weary Throat: Memoir of an American Pilgrimage* (New York: Liverlight, 2018), 460. See also "Pauli Murray Lashes Out at Back Row Role," *Afro-American*, November 23, 1963.

11 / Three Hitchhikers—and the Students Left Behind

85 "We're getting ready" and "OK": "Determined to Reach 1963 March, Teen Used Thumb and Feet," NPR.org., August 14, 2013, https://www.npr.org/2013/08/14/210470828/determined-to-reach-1963-march-teen-used-thumb-and-feet.

86 "It was brutal as hell": Henry T. Benjamin, "Police Savagery Continues Over Strife-Torn US," *Philadelphia Tribune*, June 22, 1963.

86 "Here's this man": "Determined to Reach 1963 March," August 14, 2013.

87 "Y'all are crazy": Sarrah Peters, "Avery Recalls 1963 March on Washington," *Gadsden Messenger*, no date, https://gadsdenmessenger.com/avery-recalls-1963-march-on-washington/.

87 "Washington or Bust," and "*Boom!*": Lisa Rogers, "Gadsden Teens Hitchhiked Toward History at March on Washington," *Gadsden Times*, August 25, 2013.

88 "You boys know," "Yeah," and "Y'all need": "Determined to Reach 1963 March," August 14, 2013.

89 "You are *strongly advised*": *Organizing Manual No. 2*," no date [August 1963], 10.

90 "Wow! Girls!" and "the youngest was": Rogers, "Gadsden Teens Hitchhiked," August 25, 2013.

90 "WE MARCH FOR JOBS FOR ALL NOW": The official signs can be found in numerous online sites. See part of the Smithsonian Institution's collection at https://www.si.edu/spotlight/1963-march-on-washington.

92 "I just left your hometown": Rogers, "Gadsden Teens Hitchhiked," August 25, 2013.

12 / Freedom Trains

93   "nothing short of pandemonium": Lloyd General, "2500 Jam Station Enroute to March," *Chicago Daily Defender*, August 28, 1963.

93   "This overwhelming response": Lloyd General, "A Whole Nation Will Hold Its Breath While 250,000 March," *Chicago Daily Defender*, August 27, 1963.

93   "trying to make": Michael Drapa and Max Witynski, "Timuel Black, Civil Rights Leader and Chicago Historian, 1918–2021," *UChicago News*, October 13, 2021, https://news .uchicago.edu/story/timuel-black-civil-rights-leader-and-chicago-historian-1918-2021.

96   "I hope this train" and "It means an opportunity": "Studs Terkel's 1963 Train Ride to Washington," WBEZ Chicago, January 16, 2015, https://www.wbez.org/stories/studs -terkels-1963-train-ride-to-washington/a2dc75ea-2529-40f2-b801-46ac4d04e1d4.

96   "This train is bound for glory": Musicians have used many different lyrics for this song. The origins of the version sung by Etta Moton Barnett are unclear.

96–97   "And this train is bound for Washington," "some jobs," "I've seen," "I could never," "wonderful," and "If every white man": "Studs Terkel's 1963 Train Ride to Washington," January 16, 2015.

97   "So you're down here": Evan Thomas, *Robert Kennedy: His Life* (New York: Simon & Schuster, 2013), 263 (digital version).

13 / SNCC Pickets, Malcolm Pokes

99   "The Justice Department Is": "Chanting Civil Rights Marchers," *Minneapolis Star*, August 28, 1963.

100   "walked four blocks": James Forman, *The Making of Black Revolutionaries* (Seattle: University of Washington Press, 1997), 339.

100   "It must have been": Forman, *The Making of Black Revolutionaries*, 341.

102   "When There Is No Justice": Bryce Wilson Stucki, "Moses of Mississippi," *American Prospect*, August 20, 2013.

103   "were going to the march" and "angry in mood": John D. Due, "At March on Washington: The Anger, the Fear, the Love and the Hope," CNN.com, September 1, 2013, https://www.cnn.com/2013/08/24/opinion/due-march-on-washington-memories.

103–4   "been taken over" and "Had he freed": "Says Abe Didn't Free Negro Race," *Clarion-Ledger* (Jackson, MS), August 27, 1963.

104   "seeking favors from": Michael Pakenham, "Rights Marchers Are Sightseers, Too!" *Chicago Tribune*, August 29, 1963.

104   "fiasco": "9,000-Man Law Force on Alert," *Miami Herald*, August 28, 1963.

104   "an explosion" and "pushed around": Edward McGrath, "Nation's Capital Tense but Ready for Massive Civil Rights March," *Boston Globe*, August 28, 1963.

104   "dead man's statue": "Says Abe Didn't Free Negro Race," August 27, 1963.

104   "all-black": Pakenham, "Rights Marchers Are Sightseers, Too," August 29, 1963.

104   "a federal civil rights police force": Frank Van Der Linden, "Despite Kennedy Claims Thurmond Cites Leftist Ties Among March Groups," *Nashville Banner*, July 26, 1963.

14 / Militant Voices

107   "John, come downstairs" and "It's your speech": Lewis with D'Orso, *Walking with the Wind*, 221.

107–8   "In good conscience," "revolution," and "We will march": Lewis with D'Orso, *Walking with the Wind*, 219–221.

108   "patience" and "To those who have said": Lewis with D'Orso, *Walking with the Wind*, 220.

108   "This is offensive" and "by the time": Lewis with D'Orso, *Walking with the Wind*, 222.

109–10   "I think the biggest influence," "I don't think," "[A]s far as I'm concerned," "The white power structure," "I want to go," "If this thing," "We don't trust you," and "We've been stabbed": Marlene Nadle, "March on Washington: The View from the Front of the Bus," *Village Voice*, September 5, 1963, posted June 4, 2020, https://www.villagevoice.com/2020/06/24/march-on-washington-the-view-from-the-front-of-the-bus/.

113   "Freedom-Now!": Karl L. Young, "Man About Town," *Michigan Chronicle*, September 7, 1963.

15 / Rising at Dawn

118   "We cannot maintain order": Euchner, *Nobody Turn Me Around*, 8.

119   "Gentlemen, everything is going": Jervis Anderson, *Bayard Rustin: Troubles I've Seen* (New York: HarperCollins, 1997), 255.

119   "O Lord, be with us": Harry Ferguson, "A Prayer Is Answered—'He Had the Whole March in His Hands,'" *Chicago Defender*, August 31, 1963.

120–21   "crucial difference": Ben A. Franklin, "Rights Marchers to Strain Capital," *New York Times*, August 12, 1963.

121   "We are here on behalf": "Ring of Police Is Put Around Group of Nazis," *Herald Statesman* (Yonkers, New York), August 28, 1963.

121   "My men will aid": Richard Starnes, "'We Are Soldiers of the Army,' Sing Teenagers in Demonstration," *El Paso Herald-Post*, August 28, 1963.

121–23   "the mood was one," "You can never know," and "Now that's what I call": "Marchers Sing and Voice Hope on Way to Washington Rally," *New York Times*, August 28, 1963.

123–24   "The Washington March of Aug. 28": "An Appeal by the March Leaders," no date, Social Welfare Project (online), Virginia Commonwealth University Libraries, http://socialwelfare.library.vcu.edu/wp-content/uploads/2010/12/an_appeal_by_march_leaders.jpg.

124   "walk": "Citizens Abroad 'Walk' for U.S. Civil Rights," *Chicago Defender*, August 24, 1963.

124   "We want to serve notice": "Civil Rights March Planned by 50 Americans in Paris," *New York Times*, August 18, 1963.

16 / The Occupation Begins

125   "Well, whatever Black folks do": Ossie Davis, interviewed by Madison Davis Lee, July 6, 1989. This interview was conducted for the documentary series *Eyes on the Prize: America at the Crossroads, 1965–1985*, produced by Blackside, Inc., http://repository.wustl.edu /concern/videos/3b591d21z.

129   "little old ladies": Jean Shepherd, "The Jean Shepherd Show," WOR AM, New York, New York, August 29, 1963, https://archive.org/details/TheJeanShepherdShowWORAM 19630829MarchOnWashingtonEdit.

129   "the downtown streets" and "For the natives": Russell Baker, "Capital Is Occupied by a Gentle Army," *New York Times*, August 29, 1963.

129   "What are you" and "I guess so": Krissah Thompson, "In March on Washington, White Activists Were Largely Overlooked but Strategically Essential," *Washington Post*, August 25, 2013.

130   "Florestine, this is what": Jonathan Eig, *King: A Life* (New York: Farrar, Straus and Giroux, 2023), chapter 27 (329).

131   "family reunion" and "holiday mood": Shepherd, "The Jean Shepherd Show," August 29, 1963.

131   "Milton Wilkerson": Baker, "Gentle Army Occupies Capital," August 29, 1963.

132   "Sure, nigger, after you": Michael Thelwell, *Duties, Pleasures, and Conflicts: Essays in Struggle* (Amherst: University of Massachusetts Press, 1987), 71.

132   "Move on, move on": Baker, "Gentle Army Occupies Capital," August 29, 1963.

133   "I'm going to walk," "One of these days," "I'm going to be," and "One of these days": Calvin Trillin, "The Hours Before 'I Have a Dream,'" *New Yorker*, September 7, 1963.

17 / Black Women Speak, Hatemongers Rage

135   "Has that sign been approved?" and "It's my sign": Thelwell, *Duties, Pleasures, and Conflicts*, 70.

135   "All slogans carried": *Organizing Manual No. 2*, no date [August 1963], 10.
       "overjoyed": Malverse Nicholson, "I Marched for Freedom," *New Journal and Guide*, August 31, 1963.

137   "We are soldiers": Starnes, "'We Are Soldiers of the Army,'" August 28, 1963. This article cites only the first line in the song's first stanza; the rest of the lyrics can be found at numerous online sites, including hymnary.org. The writer and origin of the song are unclear.

137   "Oh, freedom": Gentile, *March on Washington*, 203.

138   "We did not know": Thompson, "In March on Washington, White Activists," August 25, 2013.

138   "I'm on my way": "March on Washington for Jobs and Freedom, Part 2 of 17," August 8, 1963, Open Vault, WGBH Media Library and Archives Collection [hereafter GBH Archives], https://openvault.wgbh.org/collections/march_on_washington/ern -coverage.

139   "Well, I always been": Elijah Wald, *Josh White: Society Blues* (Amherst: University of Massachusetts Press, 2000), 64.

140–41 "Let me have those seats," "You all better make it," "Are you going," and "No": Jeanne Theoharis, *The Rebellious Life of Mrs. Rosa Parks* (Boston: Beacon Press, 2013), 62–63.

141   "Ladies and gentlemen" and "Hello, friends of freedom": "March on Washington for Jobs and Freedom, Part 4 of 17," August 28, 1963, GBH Archives.

141   "Rosa Parks Day": Jennifer Scanlon, *Until There Is Justice: The Life of Anna Arnold Hedgeman* (New York: Oxford University Press, 2016), 169.

141–42 "This is indeed": "March on Washington, Part 4 of 17," GBH Archives, August 28, 1963.

142   "the white man": Starnes, "'We Are Soldiers of the Army,'" August 28, 1963.

142–43 "I'm ashamed of my race" and "We are here to protest": "Nazi Officer Defies Capital Police, Jailed," *Akron Beacon Journal*, August 28, 1963.

18 / The People Lead the Way

146   "My God, they're going": "Big Day—End and a Beginning," *Newsweek*, September 2, 1963, 20.

146   "[B]ut I figured I was": Euchner, *Nobody Turn Me Around*, 141.

147   "We were supposed": Lewis with D'Orso, *Walking with the Wind*, 223.

147   "and it was like [us] saying": "We Were There: Memories of the March on Washington," *TIME*, August 26, 2013.

147   "The crowds were too": Lewis with D'Orso, *Walking with the Wind*, 223.

147   "slow shuffle": B. M. Phillips, "If You Ask Me: 'Free . . . dom . . . Free . . . dom, NOW,'" *Afro-American*, September 7, 1963. See also James Ritch, "Chicagoans Plan Continuing Civil Rights Rallies in Washington," *Chicago Tribune*, August 29, 1963.

147   "A revolution is *supposed*": "Big Day—End and a Beginning," September 2, 1963, 20.

148   "a feeling of humanity": Shepherd, "The Jean Shepherd Show," August 29, 1963.

148   "Jim Crow Is Dead": "It DID Happen Here," *Shreveport Journal*, August 29, 1963.

148   "I'm gonna walk, walk" and "We Demand an Honest": Eugene Patterson, "In Shadow of Abe Lincoln, A Voice Shouts for Freedom," *Atlanta Constitution*, August 29, 1963.

149   "I wouldn't have missed": Woody L. Taylor, "Washington a 'Beehive' of Action," *Pittsburgh Courier*, August 31, 1963.

149   "Every step was painful" and "She became my symbol": Chuck Stone, "A Stone's Throw: The Negro Revolution Comes of Age," *Chicago Defender*, August 31, 1963.

153   "in the march itself": Trillin, "The Hours Before 'I Have a Dream,'" September 7, 1963.

153   "Ole Glory's tarnished": James Williams, "Black and White Americans Joined Hands, Hearts," *Afro-American*, September 7, 1963.

154   "Not only had I never": Gloria Steinem, *My Life on the Road* (New York: Random House, 2015), 41. Steinem's depiction of Greene's comments appear on 41–42.

155   "Strong people": SNCC Digital Gateway, "Ella Baker," no date, https://snccdigital.org /people/ella-baker/.

19 / Freedom Fighters

159   "double-crossing": Lewis with D'Orso, *Walking with the Wind*, 225. Roy Wilkins also uses "double cross" in Wilkins with Mathews, *Standing Fast*, 293.

159   "too little and too late" and "cheap political leaders": Lewis with D'Orso, *Walking with the Wind*, 219.

159   "calling for open revolution": Nelson Lichtenstein, *Walter Reuther: The Most Dangerous Man in Detroit* (New York: Basic Books, 1995), 386.

160   "We will take matters": Lewis with D'Orso, *Walking with the Wind*, 220.

160   "If John Lewis feels": Lichtenstein, *Walter Reuther*, 386.

161   "We have set up": Euchner, *Nobody Turn Me Around*, 151.

161   "John, we've come this far": Lewis with D'Orso, *Walking with the Wind*, 226.

161   "If the church people": Forman, *The Making of Black Revolutionaries*, 335.

162   "We never knew" and "[T]hey kept me from": Aamna Mohdin, "'They Couldn't Arrest Us All': Civil Rights Veteran Rutha Mae Harris on MLK, Protest and Prison," *Guardian*, September 10, 2020.

162   "I felt I was in the presence of genius": Sondra Barrett Hassan, interviewed by Kelly Navies, October 9, 2013, OHP 24, March on Washington 50th Anniversary Oral History Project, DC Public Library, Special Collections.

163–65   "I want you to know" and "The results today": "March on Washington for Jobs and Freedom, Part 5 of 17," GBH Archives, August 28, 1963.

20 / Celebrities

167   "I am a Puerto Rican" and "I support": Dave Hepburn, "In the Wings," *New York Amsterdam News*, September 7, 1963.

168–69   "indescribable tortures" and "Because there is nothing": "Brando Likens Ala. Police Treatment of Demonstrators to Tortures by Nazis," *York Daily Record* (PA), August 30, 1963.

170   "John, that doesn't sound": Lewis and D'Orso, *Walking with the Wind*, 225.

170   "revolution," "the masses," and "There's nothing wrong": Lewis and D'Orso, *Walking with the Wind*, 226.

21 / A Socialist Revolution

173   "Will Camilla Williams": Kathleen Mills, "IU's Camilla Williams Sang Anthem at King's 1963 March on Washington," *Herald-Times* (Bloomington, IN), January 20, 1988.

173–78 "My fellow Americans" and all quotations from this speech: "March on Washington for Jobs and Freedom, Part 6 of 17," GBH Archives, August 28, 1963.

179   "new concept of lobbying": *Manual No. 2*, no date [August 1963], 5.

179   "Pass the bill!": "March on Washington for Jobs and Freedom, Part 6 of 17," GBH Archives, August 28, 1963.

179   "don't have freedom": Harriet Van Horne, "Networks' Coverage of March Clear, Concise, Eminently Fair," *Evansville Press* (IN), August 29, 1963.

22 / A Tribute to Black Women

181   "Diane, you know": Olivia B. Waxman, "Her Fight for Civil Rights Was Recognized During the March on Washington's Tribute to Women—But She Wasn't Actually There," *TIME*, August 27, 2019.

181   "Fellow Americans": "March on Washington for Jobs and Freedom, Part 6 of 17," GBH Archives, August 28, 1963.

182   "I was hurt": Adelle M. Banks and Corrie Mitchell, "Memories of the March: 10 Voices Recall 1963 March on Washington," *Washington Post*, August 23, 2013.

182–83 "Mr. Randolph" and "We will kneel-in": "March on Washington for Jobs and Freedom, Part 6 of 17," GBH Archives, August 28, 1963.

184–85 "May I request," "I'm sorry," "Who else," and "Will the": "March on Washington for Jobs and Freedom, Part 6 of 17," GBH Archives, August 28, 1963.

185   "seething inside": Joseph R. Fitzgerald, *The Struggle Is Eternal: Gloria Richardson and Black Liberation* (Lexington: University Press of Kentucky, 2018), 127–128.

185   "You should raise hell": "Civil Rights Pioneer Gloria Richardson, 91, on How Women Were Silenced at 1963 March on Washington," *Democracy Now!* radio program, August 27, 2013.

185   "sit here until": Fitzgerald, *The Struggle Is Eternal*, 128.

186   "our time will someday": Douglas Brinkley, *Rosa Parks: A Life* (New York: Penguin Books, 2005), 185.

23 / A Minister Confesses, Marian Anderson Returns

187   "Protestant Pope": John Dart, "Rights Leader and Ecumenist E.C. Blake Dies," *Los Angeles Times*, August 1, 1985.

187   "partially because" and "We come": "March on Washington for Jobs and Freedom, Part 6 of 17," GBH Archives, August 28, 1963.

188   "The churches in this country": "Dr. Blake Among 283 Held in Racial Rally in Mary-land," *New York Times*, July 5, 1963.

188   "Churchgoers should stop": John Light and Julia Conley, "Meet the 1963 March on Washington Organizers: Eugene Carson Blake, Vice Chairman, Commission on Religion and Race, National Council of Churches," BillMoyers.com, July 25, 2013.

188   "I am delighted": R. Douglas Brackenridge, *Eugene Carson Blake: Prophet with Portfolio* (New York: Seabury Press, 1978), 96–97.

188–89 "these amazingly able": "March on Washington for Jobs and Freedom, Part 6 of 17," GBH Archives, August 28, 1963.

190   "My country" and "Nobody Knows": "Marian Anderson Sings to 75,000 in Open Air Recital," *Chicago Defender*, April 15, 1939.

193   "I'm not marching, just singing": "Marian Anderson in Tears as She Misses Start of Rally," *Bridgeport Post* (CT), August 29, 1963.

193   "We would like" and "Come on!": "March on Washington for Jobs and Freedom, Part 6 of 17," GBH Archives, August 28, 1963.

193   "would have been": Warren G. Harding, "Address at the Dedication of the Lincoln Memorial," May 30, 1922, https://www.presidency.ucsb.edu/documents/address -the-dedication-the-lincoln-memorial.

194   "the word that gave freedom": "Dr. Robert Moton's Address at the Dedication of the Lincoln Memorial," May 30, 1922, https://www.nps.gov/linc/learn/historyculture /motonremarks.htm.

194   "The venomous snake": J. LeCount Chestnut, "Mock Ideal of Lincoln at Memorial," *Chicago Defender*, June 10, 1922.

194   "it remains undedicated": "Opened but Not Dedicated Stands Memorial to Lincoln," *Chicago Defender*, June 10, 1922.

24 / Lewis Scorches

197   "Brother John Lewis!": "March on Washington for Jobs and Freedom, Part 6 of 17," GBH Archives, August 28, 1963.

197   "The sound of applause": Lewis with D'Orso, *Walking with the Wind*, 227.

197   "had not done": Forman, *The Making of Black Revolutionaries*, 333.

198–204 "We march today" and all other quotations from this speech: "March on Washington for Jobs and Freedom, Part 6 of 17," GBH Archives, August 28, 1963.

198   "too little and too late" and other references to deleted sections in original draft of speech: Lewis with D'Orso, *Walking with the Wind*, 227.

199   "The crowd was with me" and "The speech itself": Lewis with D'Orso, *Walking with the Wind*, 227.

204–5 "President Kennedy has offered" and "Some of us may die": "March on Washington for Jobs and Freedom, Part 6 of 17," GBH Archives, August 28, 1963.

205–6 "Above all, we pray": "Prayer at the March on Washington for Jobs and Freedom, by Rabbi Uri Miller (28 August 1963)," Open Siddur Project, January 17, 2017, https://opensiddur.org/prayers/civic-calendar/united-states/mlk-jr-day/prayer-march-washington-jobs-freedom-rabbi-uri-miller-august-28-1963/.

206 "Furthermore, we must work": "March on Washington for Jobs and Freedom, Part 7 of 17," GBH Archives, August 28, 1963.

206–7 "Who can call himself": Gentile, *March on Washington*, 236; Euchner, *Nobody Turn Me Around*, 175; and "Ahmann Speech.wmv," YouTube.com, https://www.youtube.com/watch?v=-MqXx_f_9A8.

207 "All over this land": "March on Washington for Jobs and Freedom, Part 7 of 17," GBH Archives, August 28, 1963.

25 / Mahalia Jackson Moves the Sea

209 "Do a color job," "no high dress," "Rosa Gragg," and "And that Mahalia": Lula Patterson, "It Was No High Dress Affair, Reports our Lula," *Afro-American*, September 7, 1963.

210 "Iiii've been 'buuuuked" and "And Iiii've been scorrrrned": "March on Washington for Jobs and Freedom, Part 7 of 17," GBH Archives, August 28, 1963.

210 "I just have to cry": James Booker, "March Reaction," *New York Amsterdam News*, September 7, 1963.

211 "Do you think she": Robert L. Nolan, "Freedom Songs Hail Dawn of Bright New Day," *Michigan Chronicle*, September 7, 1963.

211–12 "I wish I could sing" and all other quotations from this speech: "March on Washington for Jobs and Freedom, Part 7 of 17," GBH Archives, August 28, 1963.

26 / The Dream

213 "At this time": "March on Washington for Jobs and Freedom, Part 7 of 17," GBH Archives, August 28, 1963.

214–18 "But one hundred years" and all other quotations from this speech: Martin Luther King, Jr., "I Have a Dream," August 28, 1963, in *A Call to Conscience: The Landmark Speeches of Dr. Martin Luther King, Jr.* (New York: Warner Books, 2001), 80–88. This transcript includes audience responses in italics; we've excluded these responses in our use of the transcript. Unfortunately, King's speech does not appear on the tape and transcript provided by GBH Archives, the source that we have used for all other speeches.

214 "My Lord": "Freedom March Sidelights," *Michigan Chronicle*, September 7, 1963.

215   "the beauty of his oratory" and "He handles words": Patterson, "It Was No High Dress Affair, Reports our Lula," September 7, 1963.

215   "He's damn good": Eig, *King: A Life*, chapter 27 (334).

216   "The Negro and the Constitution" and "I intended": *The Autobiography of Martin Luther King, Jr.*, ed. Clayborne Carson (New York: Warner Books, 1988), 9–10.

217   "Dream on!" and "I see it!": "Big Day—End and a Beginning," September 2, 1963.

219   "We were on our feet": Euchner, *Nobody Turn Me Around*, 204.

27 / We Demand

221   "I want to introduce now" and "Everyone must listen": "March on Washington for Jobs and Freedom, Part 8 of 17," GBH Archives, August 28, 1963.

222–24 "Friends" and all other quotations from Rustin's comments on the demands: "March on Washington for Jobs and Freedom, Part 8 of 17," GBH Archives, August 28, 1963.

224–25 "And now, ladies and gentlemen" and all other comments about the pledge: "March on Washington for Jobs and Freedom, Part 8 of 17," GBH Archives, August 28, 1963.

225–26 "Here we are, God" and the remainder of the benediction: "March on Washington for Jobs and Freedom, Part 8 of 17," GBH Archives, August 28, 1963.

228   "Today I am proud": Louis Cassels, "March Reflected Racial Pride," *Atlanta Daily World*, September 1, 1963.

228   "feeling that on this day": Cassels, "March Reflected Racial Pride," September 1, 1963.

228   "If there were tears": Williams, "Black and White Americans," *Afro-American*, September 7, 1963.

228   "Mr. Randolph, it seems": Anderson, *Bayard Rustin*, 263.

Extra Steps

232   "Ban the Bomb": Starnes, "'We Are Soldiers of the Army,'" August 28, 1963.

233   "May we demonstrate": "Prayer at the March on Washington for Jobs and Freedom, by Rabbi Uri Miller (August 28, 1963)," Open Siddur Project, January 17, 2017.

233   "I have a dream" and "I heard you speak": Jon Meacham, *His Truth Is Marching On: John Lewis and the Power of Hope* (New York: Random House, 2020), 142.

233   "the cause of twenty million": Reg Murphy, "President Reassures 10 Leaders," *Atlanta Constitution*, August 29, 1963.

234   "the sores of American society": "Europeans Praise Discipline," *Montreal Star*, August 29, 1963.

IMAGE CREDITS

/ 101 (article): This article is reprinted with permission and courtesy of the New Journal and Guide, Norfolk, VA / 101 (photo): Bettmann via Getty Images / 102: © *Greenville News*—USA TODAY NETWORK / 103: Bettmann via Getty Images / 105: Estate of Bayard Rustin / 106: Steve Schapiro, Corbis via Getty Images / 109: Jack Clarity, NY Daily News via Getty Images / 111: Times-Picayune/New Orleans Advocate / 112 : Mississippi Department of Archives and History / 115: Frank Hurley, NY Daily News via Getty Images / 116: Courtesy of Irby C. Simpkins, Jr. / 118: Marion S. Trikosko, LOC / 120: Keystone, Hulton Archive, Getty Images / 122: Bettmann via Getty Images / 125: Hulton Archive, Getty Images / 126: Marion S. Trikosko, LOC / 127: Marion S. Trikosko, LOC / 128: National Archive, Newsmakers, Getty Images / 130: Marion S. Trikosko, LOC / 131: AP Photo / 132: Steve Schapiro, Corbis via Getty Images / 134: AP Photo / 136: Marion S. Trikosko, LOC / 137: Express Newspapers, Getty Images / 139: Rowland Scherman, USIA, National Archives / 140: © Bob Adelman / 142: Courtesy of The Jacob Rader Marcus Center of the American Jewish Archives, Cincinnati, Ohio, at americanjewisharchives.org / 143: Atlanta newspaper advertisement, August 31, 1963 / 144: Marion S. Trikosko, LOC / 146: Steve Schapiro, Corbis via Getty Images / 149: Warren K. Leffler, LOC / 150 (top): Marion S. Trikosko, LOC / 150 (bottom): Warren K. Leffler, LOC / 151 (top): Private Collection Photo © Barbara Singer, Bridgeman Images / 151 (bottom): © Bob Adelman / 152 (top): © Bob Adelman / 152 (bottom): Warren K. Leffler, LOC / 154: Marion S. Trikosko, LOC / 156: Estate of Bayard Rustin / 158: Fred W. McDarrah, MUUS Collection via Getty Images / 160: Warren K. Leffler, LOC / 163: Sipa via AP Images / 164: Warren K. Leffler, LOC / 166: Francis Miller, The LIFE Picture Collection, Shutterstock / 168: Hulton Archive, Getty Images / 171: Rowland Scherman, USIA, PhotoQuest, Getty Images / 172: Warren K. Leffler, LOC / 174:

INDEX

Note: Page references in *italics* indicate photographs.